D0945703

SURFING

SKILLS

TRAINING

TECHNIQUES

CROWOOD SPORTS GUIDES

SURFING

SKILLS

TRAINING

TECHNIQUES

Chris Nelson and Demi Taylor

THE CROWOOD PRESS

First published in 2017 by
The Crowood Press Ltd
Ramsbury, Marlborough
Wiltshire SN8 2HR

www.crowood.com

©The Crowood Press 2017

All rights reserved. No part of this publication may be reproduced or transmitted in any form or by any means,
electronic or mechanical, including photocopy, recording, or any information storage and retrieval system, without
permission in writing from the publishers.

British Library Cataloguing-in-Publication Data
A catalogue record for this book is available from the British Library.

ISBN 978 1 78500 228 1

Typeset by Sharon Dainton
Printed and bound in India by Replika Press Pvt Ltd

CONTENTS

PREFACE

Surfing will change your life. Surfing is the inspiration that gets you up in the morning – even when it's raining. Surfing is that thing that converts you into a meteorologist or at least compels you to keep pressing the refresh button on your laptop, hoping the forecast may have changed in the last two minutes and there might be surf this weekend. Surfing is that thing that turns you into an oceanographer – a studier of the tides, of swell and of changing conditions – you will have tide tables secured everywhere – in your home, in your car, in your desk.

Surfing is the thing that gives your holidays, your weekends, your waking hours a definite direction – it will make you a master negotiator when convincing friends, family and loved ones that, yes, another fortnight in Northern Scotland rather than southern Greece is just the ticket.

Surfing is that thing that connects you across the continents and across the oceans with like-minded people right across the globe. It is the thing that will make you stay up until four in the

morning to watch just one more heat of the Pipeline Pro. It is the thing that will make you realize that your body is an incredible piece of design; that your arms can paddle harder and you can hold your breath for longer than you ever thought imaginable. Surfing is the thing that will challenge you to explore your limits and to go beyond your comfort zone – whether that is firmly in the 1ft or 10ft range. Surfing is that thing you do that makes you who you are and makes you a surfer …

Sharing the stoke of surfing. (Photo: Sarah Bunt)

Right: Only a surfer knows the feeling. (Photo: Kate Czuczman)

PART I

AN INTRODUCTION TO SURFING

CHAPTER 1

GETTING STARTED
SURFING THROUGH THE YEARS

The art of stand-up wave riding has been around for hundreds, if not thousands of years. While scholars still debate the root of surfing, one thing that can be agreed upon is the lure of the ocean. There is something primordial in our attraction to it. Our coastal dwellings revolve around interactions with the sea so perhaps it was only natural that over time we would be drawn to enjoy the rise and fall of the tides and the power of breaking waves.

In South America, Peruvian fishermen returning from fishing trips out beyond the whitewater rode Caballitos de Totora – reed craft with a prominent curved bough – in through the surf. This may have been out of necessity or it may have been for the thrill of the ride, but the act can be seen depicted on pottery dating back 3,500 years.

The ancient Polynesians are widely accepted to be the pioneers of wave riding as we know it – that is catching waves on a board for the pure joy of the experience. The Polynesian art of surfing was recreational, ceremonial, cultural and communal, with evidence of the activity dating back to the fifteenth century, by which time surfing was already a well-established tradition.

Sport of Kings

Surfing is the original 'sport of kings'. In Hawaii two kinds of craft were traditionally ridden, solid 14 to 16ft long olo boards, which weighed in at 50kg and were carved from the wiliwili tree, plus the smaller 10 to 12ft long alaia boards that were made from koa wood.

Separating out the ruling classes and the 'commoner', only high ranking chiefs and nobles or Ali'i were permitted to ride the longer olo boards, using surfing to assert their prowess, strength and agility while the alaia were for everyone else. Certain surf breaks were also reserved for royalty where men and women surfed together, sharing waves, sometimes sharing boards. In the late 1770s Captain Cook's expedition arrived in Hawaii and witnessed surfing. The missionaries who arrived in Hawaii were shocked by what they saw – for them something this much fun had to be wrong and wave sliding, along with other Hawaiian cultures including hula, were soon banned.

A regal looking surfer wave riding in a style akin to the ancient Hawaiians. (Photo: Sarah Bunt)

Duke

Surfing was resurrected by a small group of surfers at Waikiki beach, spearheaded by the charismatic Duke Kahanamoku. Duke, as he was known, was an Olympic gold medal-winning swimmer. During the early twentieth century, he and a handful of friends helped set up the first wave sliding club, Da Hui Nalu, centred around Waikiki. They were the original 'beach boys' and taught many people how to surf. Duke travelled the world, touring his swimming and surfing exhibitions and introducing the sport of surfing to mainland USA as well as Australia. A statue of Duke stands at Waikiki beach today in honour of his achievements.

Tom Blake revolutonized surfing with his lighter more manoeuvrable designs. (Photo: Kate Czuczman)

Tom Blake

In 1920 a young Tom Blake met Duke at one of his swimming events in Detroit, USA. This meeting would change Blake's life and the course of surf history. In 1921 Blake tried surfing on the California coast and became hooked. He moved to Hawaii and immersed himself in the beach boy lifestyle. Blake was an innovator; he pioneered a hollow surfboard design, lighter than the traditional solid design. He also invented the skeg (the first fins) that made boards easier to turn and trim. In order to capture images from the line-up he produced the first camera water housing, transforming the way we see surfing. Blake was fascinated with Hawaiian culture, he dressed in loose baggy shorts and canvas shoes, helping instigate a utilitarian surf style of dress still popular today.

Traditional solid redwood boards were heavy and difficult to turn. Inspired by Blake's ideas, new board designs began to appear – surfboards became smaller and started to be made from lighter materials such as balsa wood and fibreglass, using techniques learned from the aircraft industry in the post-war era. These boards evolved into a design that would be recognizable today as the classic Malibu or longboard – around 10ft in length with rounded noses and a single large fin. Through the early 1950s surfing established vibrant communities based around the heartlands of Oahu in Hawaii, Malibu in California and east coast Australia.

Malibu and Gidget

Over the course of the 1950s it is estimated that the surfing population of California exploded from around 3,000 to close to 100,000. Much of this boom was down to one girl. In the late fifties a young misfit called Kathy Kohner visited Malibu with her newly acquired surfboard. Initially mocked by the tight-knit local crew – she was christened Gidget, a nickname combining 'girl' and 'midget' due to her short stature – she soon became accepted due to her dogged determination to learn to surf.

Kohner's Hollywood producer father listened to the stories his daughter told him about her experiences as part of the surf scene based around the point break. He pulled them together into a book and produced a film called *Gidget*. This was the first mainstream movie that explored the beach and surf lifestyle and proved a huge hit, catapulting surfing into the spotlight and inspiring many to flock to the Malibu line-up.

In post-war USA, fuelled by new found freedoms and rock 'n' roll, youth culture was beginning to blossom and for the first time teenagers were finding their own way to look and behave that differentiated them from their parents. The new wave of surfing fed into that. Surf culture had its own vernacular and lingo, surfers dressed in a distinct way and grew out their short back and sides. It was a distinct youth movement that rebelled against the social mores of the

Taking inspiration from 1950s movie Gidget. *(Photo: Sarah Bunt)*

surfboard manufacturers such as Bilbo and Bickers who were producing craft for the fledgling surf communities of Cornwall, Devon and beyond. Soon Gul Wetsuits would be founded as surfing became a national culture, with outposts quickly established in Wales, the North-east as well as Scotland.

The Endless Summer

In 1966 Bruce Brown's now iconic *The Endless Summer* became the first surf documentary to gain a national release in America. The movie followed surfers Robert August and Mike Hynson as they traversed the globe, chasing the endless summer by moving with the seasons from the USA to Africa, then Australia, New Zealand, the Pacific and Hawaii, before returning to California. The idea was simple and, with its easy nature and Brown's accessible humour, garnered mainstream attention, catching hold in the collective imagination.

By the time the film was released the shortboard era was just around the corner, but the concept of the perfect wave waiting around the next headland became ingrained at the very core of surf culture, instilling a wanderlust that exists to this day. Surfers took up the vanguard of global exploration, opening up new destinations, which until then were considered wild and remote. Pioneering locations such as Indonesia, Central America, Africa and isolated Pacific atolls, this new breed of seekers jumped aboard leaking ferries and rode dilapidated mopeds deep into the heart of malaria-riddled jungles in search of the next perfect wave. Wherever surfers landed and broken boards were discarded so the seeds were planted for a burgeoning surf community that would eventually flourish.

time and of their parents. They drove cars salvaged from scrapyards, butchering spare parts to produce the first hot rods – some factions even took it to the extreme, donning German army trench coats in a period when the Second World War was still fresh in their parents' memories.

The explosion in popularity following the success of *Gidget* saw backyard shapers inundated with more orders for surfboards than they could handle – boards were crafted by hand in a labour-intensive method. They rapidly organized themselves into crude factories and expanded into brands with a number of shapers and glassers. Companies such as Hobie, Bing, Dewey Weber, Velzy, Jacobs and Greg Noll Surfboards began sponsoring riders and producing branded T-shirts.

The Rise of the Brand

Surfboard manufacturers were by now producing polyurethane foam boards, replacing the increasingly rare and expensive balsa. Light and easily manufactured, polyurethane foam blanks were shaped and glassed to make boards weighing around 25lb, significantly lighter than balsa boards, which weighed upwards of 35lb.

Iconic surfers of this golden era included Mickey Dora, Phil Edwards, Mickey Munoz, Butch Van Artsdalen, Mike Doyle, Lance Carson and Greg Noll. As the surf spots around Malibu became increasingly congested, new breaks were pioneered to the north and south, while the lifestyle that had already established bridgeheads on the Eastern seaboard and in Europe and South Africa began to expand.

By the mid-1960s the UK had local

In search of the endless summer. (Photo: Kate Czuczman)

as Nat Young and Wayne Lynch showed the world what these boards could do and the whole surfing style changed. Longboards became obsolete, old brands struggled to change quickly enough and many of the giants went bust. This was an incredibly creative time in surf history, where cross-pollination of ideas ran back and forth with each visit from Lennox Head and Angourie in Australia to Rincon in California or Hawaii's Oahu, where Dick Brewer had been experimenting with mini guns that could take on the hollow waves of the North Shore. The single fin shortboard became the performance marque – surfing was now in the pocket and in the barrel, new carves and turns were possible. Imagination was the only limiting factor in design and backyard shapers were the new pioneers.

Chasing the Curl

The wider impact of *The Endless Summer* cannot be underestimated. It inspired a new influx into the lifestyle. Surfing became cemented as a true youth culture, drawing in inspiration from other countercultural movements. As hair grew longer so boards became shorter. During the late 1960s the length of surfboards dropped almost overnight from 9–10ft to 6–7ft. It took a quantum leap in thinking and design, pioneered by two visionaries – American surf maverick George Greenough and Australian surfer/shaper Bob McTavish. Greenough was somewhat reclusive, a mat surfer and kneeboarder who rode short spoon boards with a huge raked, flexible fin based on the tail of a tuna. This allowed him to ride in the pocket, the critical part of the wave, and even in the barrel at a time when surfers were 'trimming' their longboards out on the face. Greenough showed McTavish a surfboard he'd shaped that incorporated some of his revolutionary ideas and the potential blew McTavish's mind, inspiring him to shape a shortboard using some of Greenough's ideas. The shortboard era was born.

Back in Australia, surf champions such

Free Ride Era

During the early 1970s surfing was split between the freewheeling surf drifters

Xcel rider Kevin Schulz flying on his Rusty surfboard. (Photo: Tim McCraig/Xcel)

blown onward in search of new exciting waves and those who aspired to be successful on the IPS tour – an informal circuit set up in 1976 by the fledgling governing body, International Professional Surfers. Movies such as *Morning of the Earth* inspired a generation to hit the road, while films such as *Free Ride* captured the growing rivalries of Wayne 'Rabbit' Bartholomew, Shaun Tomson, Mark Richards, Peter Townend and Ian Cairns. This cohort of young Australians and South Africans arrived in Hawaii for the winter season of 1975–76 and shook up the old surfing order.

In the latter half of the 1970s Australian surfer Mark Richards watched Hawaiian surfer/shaper Reno Abellira

riding a stubby two-finned surfboard and the vision inspired him to produce a longer, slicker twinnie. Richards piloted the twin fin to numerous contest wins and suddenly the design caught on, proving to be more manoeuvrable than a single fin, allowing Richards to pull off more critical turns than had been seen previously. He went on to secure four consecutive world titles from 1979 to 1982.

In 1981 another Australian surfer, Simon Anderson, revolutionized surfing overnight with his three-fin thruster, winning the prestigious Bells Beach Pro contest on his new design. Anderson called the board 'the thruster' due to the drive it generated through turns. It

became the dominant board design over the next three decades, still proving to be the most popular fin set-up today.

Power Surfing

In 1982 former world tour surfer Ian Cairns founded the ASP, the Association of Surfing Professionals, as a replacement for a floundering IPS and competitive surfing took off with an ever-increasing number of world tour events taking place across the globe, from the US, Hawaii and Australia to South Africa, Europe and Japan. Some 100,000 people packed Huntington Beach in California for the OP Pro and with surf brands becoming

The generation of power surfers loved big barrelling waves. (Photo: Ocean and Earth)

multinational clothing corporations, big money deals were soon being signed by the top riders. Australian Tom Carroll became the first surfer to pen a million dollar contract with sponsors Quiksilver.

The eighties was an era dominated by legends such as Tom Curren, Tom Carroll, Mark 'Occy' Occhilupo, Damian Hardman and Gary Elkerton, and power surfing was the dominant style. Surfers were rewarded for big turns, gauging cutbacks and massive off the tops that generated huge rooster tails of spray.

New Skool

In the 1950s surfing had created skateboarding, or sidewalk surfing, in its image – as a prodigal son for dog days and flat days. By the early 1990s surfboards had become smaller and lighter and skating offered up fresh inspiration; progressive surfers such as Christian Fletcher and Martin Potter brought moves including the aerial from the skate ramps into the water. Soon after, a young Floridian surfer by the name of Kelly Slater emerged on to the scene and the 'new skool' was born. The likes of Slater, Rob Machado and Shane Herring were pioneers of this movement, riding 'banana boards' – thin, light boards with lots of nose and a tail 'rocker' adding curve to their length. The speedy and snappy surfing in small waves pushed possibilities – tails were spun out further into tailslides, a cutback turned into an opportunity to ride out backwards.

This fresh intake of young surfers started a generational battle between those that excelled with speed, power and flow and those that brought new manoeuvres into the small wave stops on the tour. What few foresaw was that this new intake would also charge hard in the big, powerful waves of Hawaii, ringing in a changing of the guard.

Kelly Slater quickly rose to become the best surfer on the planet. He won an unprecedented six world titles before retiring in 1998. But it wasn't just the men making waves in the water and Lisa Andersen truly put women's surfing on to the main stage by winning her fourth consecutive world title in 1997.

The Dream Tour and Slater's Return

The world tour had come of age – out went the small wave grovel stops like Huntington Beach and Lacanau in came the best waves on the planet, the 'Dream Tour'. The Superbank, Bells Beach, Cloudbreak, J-Bay, Teahupoo, Hossegor and Pipeline were all on the roster. With the surfing rather than the spectator numbers at the forefront Kelly Slater was inspired to come out of retirement, fired by a rivalry with up and coming Hawaiian surfer Andy Irons. The two had an intense competitive battle, with Irons claiming three world titles and Slater going on to take his career total to eleven.

The Air Game

Where Fletcher and Pottz pioneered and Slater pushed, the next generation took it to another level. Originally airs were straight, small wave fare, rarely landed. This new generation took up the gauntlet and pushed surfing high above the lip in all conditions and all breaks. John Florence, Kolohe Andino, Filipe Toledo, Josh Kerr, Dane Reynolds and Julian Wilson smashed the boundaries, proving they had the ability to perform in all waves – Pipe barrel to huge mute 360s? No problem.

ASP Tour becomes the WSL

The Association of Surfing Professionals (ASP) era was dominated by Kelly Slater. He became the first wave rider to cross over and garner true mainstream fame,

The era of aerials continues to inspire young surfers today. (Photo: Xcel)

gracing broadsheets the world over and making the cover of GQ magazine in 2011 in an edition devoted to the '25 coolest athletes of all time'. In 2015 the ASP became the World Surfing League (WSL) in a bid by the new governing body to take surfing into a more mainstream and professional position in line with football and baseball, thus widening its appeal. It was fitting then that the final ASP World Champion was Brazilian Gabriel Medina, helping to underline the ambition of making surfing truly global. Co-ordinating events including the Championship Tour, Qualifying Series as well as the Longboard Tour and Big Wave Awards, the contests are streamed live on the web, commentated on by a panel of experts.

Surfing's World Domination and Diversification

Meanwhile, in line-ups across the globe surfers have begun to embrace their heritage, riding an increasingly diverse range of boards and finding fun in mastering the techniques required to get the most out of these craft. From 1970s-inspired single fins through to bonzers and finless alaias, the line-up has never seen a more varied spectrum of wave riding vehicles as it does today.

Away from the media spotlight of contests, wave riding has developed into a rich and diverse culture with an all-encompassing lifestyle. Surfers now ride a wider range of boards than ever, in more

places than ever. There are surf communities everywhere from Alaska to Russia, from China to the smallest Pacific atoll. It is rare that a good swell goes unridden anywhere in the world.

In the UK alone there are more than 600,000 year-round surfers, and the lifestyle keeps growing. In May 2012 The Economist website reported that the number of surfers (people who claim to surf at least once a year) worldwide grew from 26 million in 2001 to 35 million in 2011. A recent report by Global Industry Analysts Inc. estimated that the world surfing market would reach US$13.2 billion by 2017, up from US$6.24 billion in 2010.

Surfing is the new wave, and everyone wants to ride it …

Leah Dawson embracing surfing's heritage on her retro-inspired single fin. (Photo: Kate Czuczman)

More people than ever are surfing in the UK. (Photo: Sarah Bunt)

Where old meets new. A longboarder and shortboarder showing their skills. (Photo: Sarah Bunt)

CHAPTER 2

SURFING STYLES

Surf conditions are in a constant state of flux due to the fluid nature of tide, wind and swell meaning no two waves are ever the same. As a result, the art of surfing can be considered fairly subjective, heavily weighted towards style.

Surfing style has altered massively through the years, evolving with equipment changes and a progressive drive to push the boundaries of performance wave riding. Manoeuvres pioneered by the professional elite filter down into the line-up and the standard rises every year.

Through this, three main schools have emerged in both competitive and free-surfing: they are longboard, shortboard and big wave.

World Surf League Disciplines

Longboard

Longboards stem from the early days of modern surfing when boards were traditionally more than 9ft long and of either of balsa and fibreglass or foam and fibreglass construction.

Traditional longboards can be anything from 9ft long to more than 10ft and have a large single fin. They are wide and stable, can be knee-paddled, are steady in the trim and are perfect platforms for old-school manoeuvres such as walking the board, cross stepping,

Ben Skinner hanging ten on the nose of his longboard. (Photo: Sarah Bunt)

nose rides/hang tens and drop knee turns.

Progressive longboards are thinner, lighter and usually have more than one fin – often three. They are usually only 9ft (the length at which a board is officially classed as a longboard) and much more manoeuvrable. They are designed to be ridden more like a shortboard, easier to cut back and perform vertical snaps, off the lips and even barrel ride. This technique has been at the centre of competitive logging for many years, but criteria are changing in response to the increasing popularity of the traditional ways.

World Surf League rules dictate that the minimum length of longboard required for WSL sanctioned

competition is 9ft (measured nose to tail) with a minimum aggregate width of 47in (a combination of the widest point of the board plus the width 12in from the nose and 12in from the tail).

The competition scene has recently seen old-school longboarding styles come back into vogue with the highest scores awarded to those who perform controlled manoeuvres in the most critical section of the waves using the full length of the board with style, flow and grace, with an emphasis on extended nose-riding, rail surfing, cross stepping and footwork as well as speed and power. This change in focus away from progressive longboarding in competition reflects the trend in line-ups across the world that has seen a resurgence of

A stylish 'stretch five' from longboarder Kassia Meador. (Photo: Kate Czuczman)

classic styles and a growth in the popularity of 'logging'.

Shortboard

Shortboarding, as the name would suggest, involves riding a shorter board. However, it is not constrained by the same sort of equipment parameters as longboarding, so the range of surfboards available and styles reflects this. In general terms, a shortboard is usually 5–7ft in length with the size and dimensions of your shortboard relative to your height, weight and skill level as well as your particular surfing style. In terms of competitive surfing, key elements considered by the judges include how innovative, difficult and progressive your manoeuvres are, along with your commitment to them plus speed, power and flow. It is more about riding the wave

and less about riding the board. This criteria, combined with the conditions on the day, will affect board selection with most pro surfers riding traditional pointed-nosed shortboards with either a classic three-fin thruster or four-fin quad set-up.

The elite World Championship Tour showcases the best shortboarders on the planet in some of the best surf locations. The championship is battled out in heats of four, three or two surfers competing against one another, selecting the best waves where they can showcase their arsenal of manoeuvres on the wave face, in the barrel and in the air. Each stop on the tour offers up different wave characteristics – for example massive barrels at Pipeline in Hawaii or large open faces at Bells Beach, Australia – and as a result the type of manoeuvres that

will score most highly at each event will alter.

Looking around an average line-up it is clear that classic thrusters are still the most popular craft. However, an increasing number of alternative designs are present, creating three main camps in the shortboard realm.

Stylist

This classic style of riding uses power and flow, linking turns with smooth arcs, maintaining momentum, taking a high line and generating speed through the rise and fall along the face. This evolved with the shortboard revolution of the late 1960s and makes the most of the characteristics of the single fin, mid-length, fish and mini-Simmons type of boards.

These boards tend to have more

volume and carry more speed, however the fin set-ups create less drive through a turn than a performance thruster. This leads to more speed into a turn, however in order to carry the momentum, a surfer must perform a curved cutback maintaining the flow. Being smooth is rewarded.

Power Surfing

During the 1980s a new brand of surfing came to the fore, known as power surfing. This harnessed the new performance characteristics that the thruster delivered, bringing in critical hacking turns throwing lots of spray. Cutting edge surfing became focused on big vertical snaps and explosive top turns.

Surfers such as Tom Curren brought a smooth style into the thruster era, mixing the vertical approach with smooth bottom turns carrying lots of speed. Others took to a more aggressive all-out power surfing style – surfers such as Tom Carroll, Gary Elkerton and Sunny Garcia.

Power surfing has never really gone out of fashion. There is always an appreciation of speed and power, of drive through turns and of explosive and dynamic off the tops with large fans of spray.

Progressive

Modern Progressive surfing has been built on the foundations of the Nu-Skool movement that came in the 1990s with Kelly Slater and co. pushing small, light boards past their limits – going beyond vertical, busting the fins out, sliding the tail and drifting.

This form of riding pushes the envelope of surfing, embracing skate-inspired aerials, often incorporating above the lip spins and grabs. These moves are made possible by the small, lightweight thruster that is super responsive and can generate speed easily, no longer relying on maintaining momentum. This allows 'angular' turns and aggressive changes of direction – accompanied by sheets of spray.

Shaun Skilton displaying his power surfing. (Photo: Sarah Bunt)

Big Wave

Big wave surfing is very much a specialist realm. Here, size is everything. It's less about critical manoeuvres and more about surviving monstrous drops. The big wave realm begins to kick in at the 15–20ft range and can go upward of 60ft faces. As a result it requires a different skill and mindset to take on these massive mountains of water, not to mention a dedicated team including a buddy on a personal water craft (PWC) who is usually on hand to support these big wave riders. Big wave surfers are committed to the pursuit of riding the biggest swells across the globe from Mavericks in California to Nazare in Portugal and Jaws in Hawaii, to name just a few.

There are a number of independent big wave contests. Due to the nature of the beast and the requirement of epic swells to create the largest of waves, big wave surf contests usually have 'waiting

An impressive above the lip display from Sam Lamiroy. (Photo: Sarah Bunt)

periods' of a number of months during which the competition can be called 'on'. The Big Wave Tour has recently been brought under the WSL umbrella and the judging criteria rewards commitment, intensity and size of wave, degree of difficulty as well as control and manoeuvres. Alongside this, the Big Wave Awards reward those men and women who have taken on the biggest waves of the year across the globe, with prize money awarded to the surfers, photographers and filmmakers who have captured these awesome feats and submitted them to the contest. Categories include Ride of the Year, Paddle Award – awarded to the surfer who paddles themselves into and rides the biggest wave of the year, Tube Award for the biggest barrel and – perhaps the one that draws the most views – the Wipe Out Award.

Big wave surfer and Xcel rider Greg Long taking off on a monster wave. (Photo: Frank Quirarte/Xcel)

CHAPTER 3

CONSTRUCTION OF A SURFBOARD

The structure of a surfboard is a lot more complex that it first appears. It's a construction that is rooted in the technology that came out of the Second World War arms race. Many hours of skilled work go into shaping and glassing a board, an artisan craft that is still largely done by hand. A board takes about a week to make from start to finish, allowing for glassing.

A surfboard has a core that provides the float. In essence this light core is fragile and porous so is protected by a strong waterproof coating. This process is known as lamination. During this process the glasser will cover the shaped blank with fibreglass sheet. These can vary in thickness, typically being a light 4oz or a heavier and therefore tougher 6oz, or a board may have an 8oz deck patch where it needs the most protection from potential damage caused by a surfer's heels and knees. The core is wrapped in the fibreglass cloth, then a liquid resin is poured over the top. First the laminate coat (which saturates the cloth) is laid on, this is followed by the second – the hot coat – and finally the third – the gloss coat. Each layer is left to harden before the next is applied and the end result is a tough outer shell.

Originally modern surfboards used a light wood called balsa, a fragile and buoyant material for the core. However, during the post-war period balsa became increasingly scarce and expensive. Surfers who had been involved in the aircraft industry began using a new material they had used in plane construction called polyurethane foam (PU). PU foam blocks could be easily shaped and sanded, prior to lamination with a polyester resin. Despite the fact that the blanks and resins are petrochemical-based and environmentally questionable, this is still the way the majority of surfboards are produced to this day.

A new core material that is becoming increasingly popular due to its better environmental credentials is expanded polystyrene (EPS). EPS blanks can be produced from recycled packing materials. These blanks also benefit from being lighter than traditional PU blanks but are harder to shape, so more time consuming. EPS blanks also need to be laminated but require a different resin as polyester dissolves the polystyrene, so they are glassed with an epoxy resin.

EPS boards have a lot more air in them and need a vent to allow for air expansion, not only when taking a hot board into a cold ocean but also when taking one on an aeroplane.

Board Design Elements

There are many elements that a shaper will work into a surfboard design.

Jamie Ward throwing some spray on his polyurethane foam board. (Photo: Sarah Bunt)

Plan Shape or Template

This is the outline of the surfboard, a symmetrical curve that runs from the nose to tail and back to the nose. The plan shape incorporates many, but not all, the important design elements of a board such as the width of the nose, the width of the board at its 'wide point', and the outline of the tail. The wide point of a surfboard affects the way the board handles. In older single-fin boards the wide point tended to be forward of the middle, whereas in performance shortboards the wide point is closer to the tail where the surfer stands.

Volume and Length

The length and volume of a surfboard will greatly affect the way it handles. A board with more volume will float better, be more stable to paddle and catch waves easier.

However, there is a balance, as a board with more volume tends to be less manoeuvrable.

A longer board tends to catch waves easier than a shorter board, however this again is one element that makes a board less responsive and harder to turn than a smaller one. Longboards and big wave guns generally catch waves better than high performance shortboards.

Nose

Longboards traditionally had rounded noses and with the shorter boards came more pointed noses, a tradition that remained with the majority of shortboards until the end of the 2000s. With new designs came boards inspired by the mini-Simmons style of craft, which had rounded noses. The majority of performance thrusters now have less pointed noses than previously.

Rails

The rounded edge of a board will help determine how it handles in the steep part of the wave as well as how it runs. There are 50/50 rails, down-rails and sharp rails. The contours of rails can change from nose to tail, with 50/50 rails in the middle of the board to ease turns, through to sharp rails in the tail to provide drive and bite in a turn.

Rocker

This is the curve in a board when looked at from the side. There is a nose rocker – how much the nose curves up – and tail rocker – how much the tail curves up. This curve through the board helps the board turn in critical manoeuvres. A board with less rocker is faster as there is less resistance to the board moving through the water. Overall the curve through a board is known as the foil.

Bottom Contour

As well as there being a slight rocker, the bottom of the surfboard can have a number of contours that affect the way it performs and can be specially tailored for the type of waves to be ridden or for how a surfer would like to ride them:

- A Vee bottom or hull has a very subtle convex V – like the hull of boat, although it is barely noticeable to the naked eye. If you take a ruler and hold the flat edge at 90 degrees to the stringer, you will be able to see the bottom contour more easily. Reverse Vee is a subtle V carved into the base running from nose to tail, creating airflow through the middle of the board.
- A single concave is a subtle curve that runs from rail to rail through the length of the board, meaning there is a channel from nose to tail.
- A double concave board has two smooth channels running nose to tail.

It is also possible to tune the way a board performs by combining bottom contours, so a board could have a Vee through the nose leading into a single

'Minnow' Green riding a longboard with its classic rounded nose. (Photo: Sarah Bunt)

Sarah Bentley hitting the lip on her parabolic board. (Photo: Sarah Bunt)

concave through the middle and then into a double concave through the tail.

Stringer

The stringer is a strip of wood that runs nose to tail through the middle of a surfboard. The stringer helps to add strength and is built into the foam as the blank is being made. Most surfboards have one stringer but some longboards have three, the two extra ones running parallel to the central one about halfway between it and the rails. In recent years the parabolic stringer has been developed, whereby the strengthening is positioned along the rails with the wood being bent into an arc and then glued to the blank. This adds a higher performance flex pattern to the board while maintaining its strength.

Tail

The shape of the tail has a huge bearing on the way a surfboard performs in different conditions. A wide tail provides a lot of drive in smaller waves, a narrow tail is better for stability in steeper waves where drive is less crucial and 'bite' is more important. The width of the tail is combined with the tail shape. A square tail has squared off corners, a squash tail is a square tail with rounded off corners, a round tail is as it sounds – rounded or oval in shape, and a swallow tail has a V carved out so it terminates in two points. A pin tail is typical of a board for larger waves and has a slightly rounded point. A swallow tail allows a wider tail where the fins are placed for more drive, but has less resistance through a turn than a comparable squash tail. The squash tail is the most popular tail for thrusters as it is a compromise for all conditions and therefore perfect for the surfer who only has one board in his or her quiver.

Stingers/Hips

Stingers and hips are steps in the rail, usually behind the two side fins on a thruster set up. These allow a board to retain width through the area where the back foot goes, giving drive and helping to generate speed in smaller waves, while the resulting reduction in area behind the

Marcus Lascelles takes to the air on his squash-tailed thruster. (Photo: Sarah Bunt)

Surfboards need to be both strong and light. (Photo: Sarah Bunt)

called 'high-aspect ratio fins' based on a template from the tail fins of a bluefin tuna. Greenough had a great grasp of aerodynamics (the forces of drag upon the leading edge of the wing or fin are countered by the degree or 'ratio' that they are swept back – the 'aspect'). The Greenough fin allowed a board leverage through a turn so it could be carved rather than just 'steered' as with old school longboard 'D' shaped skegs.

There are many elements that affect the way a fin performs and how it affects the way a board handles. The template of a fin depends upon the overall area of the fin and the height, width of the base and the amount of rake – or curve.

The foil is the cross section of the fin and affects how water flows across it, just as the cross section of a wing affects air flow. On a single fin the foil is symmetrical in cross section, whereas in the thruster each fin is unique and must be placed in the correct place. The two forward fins have a greater curve – and hence surface area – on their outer edge, whereas the trailing fin is symmetrical as with a single fin. Foil helps produce lift but also generates drag, so as with all aspects of hydrodynamics on a surfboard, it is all about balance. Flex depends on the stiffness of a fin; a stiff fin provides stability through turns but tends to create more drawn out turns. A more flexible fin allows for sharper turns but is less stable.

Fin Set-ups

Boards originally had one fin, fixed near the tail along the axis of the stringer. This is a single fin set-up, common on many longboards and mid-lengths, but also on some shortboards. In the late 1970s professional surfer Mark Richards pioneered a twin-fin set-up of two smaller fins, either side of the stringer close to the rails. The 'twinnie' proved to be more manoeuvrable than single fins,

hips means less resistance in turns. They are often used in conjunction with a swallow tail to reduce the surface area of a wide board in the tail.

Fins

Fins help a board bite into the face of the wave, giving stability in a straight line and leveraging drive and torque when rising and falling along the open wave, as well as through turns.

Typically a fin looks like a raked shark fin, and in a way that is where the design has come from – or a tuna to be exact. In the 1960s a surfer called George Greenough came up with a concept and Richards won four world titles on these boards. In the early 1980s Simon Anderson came up with a three-fin design where a third fin was added towards the tail. He christened this set-up the thruster due to the superior drive generated. For the next two decades the thruster was the fin set-up of virtually all shortboards.

A quad has four fins, two each side. These boards are fast and work well in hollow waves giving superior bite, however they are less manoeuvrable than a traditional thruster. The quad set-up has increased in popularity recently and many boards now have five sets of fin plugs, allowing the flexibility that they can be ridden as thrusters or quads.

A bonzer is a five-fin set-up pioneered by the Campbell brothers of California in the early 1970s. This set-up was well ahead of the curve and featured a larger single fin, with either two or four smaller fins set either side of the stringer. These side fins are keels rather than the traditional raked foil found on twinnies and thrusters. Bonzers also incorporated a number of concave channels through the tail.

A Futures Fins thruster set. (Photo: Futures)

Fin Systems

During the construction of a surfboard fins were traditionally glassed into the board for strength and stability. Some boards incorporated fin boxes – slots glassed into the board – that allowed single fins to be taken out or swapped for different sizes, but these were the exception rather than the rule. Then in the early 1990s a company called FCS came up with a system where fin plugs were glassed into a board, and fins with corresponding plugs could slot into and be held in place by a recessed Allen key bolt. These were marketed as a way to tune the board by adding bigger or smaller fins depending upon conditions. It

also allowed fins to be removed for travelling, eliminating the problem of fins being broken during transit. This new generation of fins were designed to break at the base in the event of an impact, meaning that if snapped they could be swapped out with spares. This eliminated the need for expensive board repairs to glassed-in fins. There are many fin manufacturers on the market today with the two most dominant brands FCS and Future Fins. The FCS system uses fins with two tabs at the base that slot into corresponding holes in the base of the board. These are secured either by a keyless tensioned roller or a hexagonal bolt tightened by an Allen key. Future Fins has designed a fin box that is one long slot with fins having a single long tab at the base, secured by a single hex bolt.

Asymms

Some surfboard designers have been pushing the envelope with various exciting new concepts. Asymms or asymmetrical boards are built on the premise that surfboards do not need to be symmetrical, i.e. the rail shape, the tail and fin placement could be different on each side of the board. The theory is that we surf in a different way on our backhand to our forehand and therefore could benefit from, say, a sharper rail on our frontside for drive or a more rounded tail on our backhand to aid cutbacks. They were developed primarily on point breaks where the surfer spends virtually all his or her time riding one way, except for when cutting back.

The same theory follows with fin placement where one side of the stringer may have a conventional thruster-like fin placement, while the other side could have two fins – as in half a quad set-up.

Finless Surfboards

Original surfboards were long, thin and finless. These Hawaiian alaias were turned by trailing a foot in the face of the wave. Board design and surfing style was changed forever when Tom Blake invented the skeg, or fin, which allowed the board to turn much more easily. Today there is a new wave of surfers who are taking modern surfboard dynamics and applying them to finless surfcraft. These trim down the line at great speed due to reduced drag, as well as allowing the surfer to spin the board through 360 degrees while still moving across the wave face. This form of riding has been pioneered by former pro surfer Derek Hynd, who uses his 'far field free friction' theory. His finless boards have complex tail designs incorporating asymmetrics, channels and deep concaves.

A fun design on a classic longboard fin. (Photo: Captain Fin)

CHAPTER 4

CHOOSING A SURFBOARD

There are few areas left in modern life where you can buy a custom-made object that has been handcrafted by an expert to suit your needs perfectly. The surfboard is one exception. Here a skilled shaper will design, shape and glass a board to your personal specifications.

Fits Like a Glove

A surfboard is a wonder of design. Decades of experimentation, hydrodynamic research and fine-tuning have gone into the modern wave riding vehicle. Rail contours, tail rocker, volume, foil, nose outline, fin placement; just a few of the myriad variables that affect how each board performs. With so many elements to feed into each design, it means that every surfboard is as unique as the person who orders it; a piece of art that allows a surfer to ride a wave that has traversed an ocean to break on a beach thousands of miles away from the storm that generated it.

There are a number of questions a surfer needs to answer in order to help a shaper in the design process:

- How long have you been surfing?
- What level do you surf at – beginner, intermediate, advanced?
- What sort of waves do you surf – mellow, steep, hollow, powerful?
- How often do you surf?
- How tall are you and how much do you weigh?

The answer to each will feed into the parameters for the finished board and will affect how it performs in different conditions. For example, a long, wide board catches waves with little effort and tends to be a more stable platform, making it easier to pop up and stand on. They trim and paddle well. This makes longer, wider boards more popular with beginners and intermediate surfers. However, the bulk of the board makes it less manoeuvrable, more difficult to turn, harder to duck dive and more tricky to hold on to in the whitewater.

Once a surfer progresses, other factors begin to feed into the equation. If a board will only be used in smaller waves perhaps size will not be an issue. However, if a surfer would like to take on bigger surf where duck diving is required then they would not want to spend all their time on the inside being battered by whitewater. A shaper would tweak the board's length and volume to make it easier to duck dive and hence get out back. If a surfer will only manage to get in the sea a few times per year then paddle fitness will be a big issue. A board with more length and width is easier to paddle and therefore requires less energy and fitness to get going.

A young surfer learning on a foamie surfboard with a little assistance from Dad. (Photo: Sarah Bunt)

Foamie surfboards are perfect for learning to surf due to their stable shape and soft top. (Photo: Ocean and Earth)

Buying your First Board

There is one golden rule when buying a surfboard. Be honest about your ability and buy a board to suit you – not the board you see pros riding. Humility is important here! If you are at the beginning of your journey as a surfer this will help you on to the craft most suited to you, and help you progress on to the next level more quickly. Think about the stage you are at, how often you get in the water and the type of waves you'll be riding.

If you are in the whitewater consider hiring a foam board until you have nailed the basics. Foamies are easy to keep hold of in the turbulence of the whitewater and its soft material means you'll be less likely to get injured by the buffeted board when you fall off.

If you're at the point where you can make it out back and you're getting on to the unbroken part of a wave, then a mini-mal is probably the best craft. They are stable, catch waves well and are manoeuvrable enough to be able to turn. A good mini-mal will see a beginner through learning the basics of how to trim and how to turn.

Mini-mals also retain their value well as there is always a healthy demand from new surfers. The only drawback is that a board of this volume is harder to duck dive.

Second-hand First

It is a good idea to buy a first surfboard from a reputable shop's second-hand rack. They tend to pick up a few dings and hopefully you'll be moving on to a different board as you progress. A decent mini-mal is a sound investment and should be easy to sell on. Once the basics have been mastered and you're ready for your next board, it's time to visit the dusty shaping bay.

Buying from a Shaper

There is nothing like getting your hands on your first custom-shaped surfboard; the smell of the resin and the pristine unblemished glass. When it comes to choosing with whom to entrust this task, there are many excellent shapers in the UK. Ask around; there is bound to be a good shaper near you if you live on the coast. If not, check out online who has made boards that you like.

There are so many elements that influence the type of craft you need and a good shaper will help you distil these down into a finished board that fits your needs and helps you make the most of the waves you surf, maximizing your fun. Discuss the level of surfing that you're at, the breaks you frequent, what types of waves and where you'd like to be with your surfing moving forward. The process will lead to a board tailored to your exact needs and the waves you'll be riding for little more than the price of one you could buy off the shelf.

A surfer mastering the basics on a mini-mal. (Photo: Sarah Burt)

CHOOSING A SURFBOARD

Beach Beat has been making surfboards in the UK since 1986. (Photo: Sarah Bunt)

Buying 'Off The Rack'

Many shops carry stock boards and a good surf shop can advise on one that will fit your requirements. There has never been a more varied selection available than today. These range from artisan custom-made resin-tinted single fin boards from famous Californian shapers, through to 'cheap as chips' Chinese or Thai imports. If a brand new surfboard is considerably cheaper than that of a local shaper, it's worth asking yourself why that might be. Chinese imports are often machine cut by workers on low pay, who may have never seen the sea. There are already low margins in board sales, but imports from China have driven down board prices. A surfboard is probably the most important purchase you make as a surfer – it's worth thinking long and hard about

the board you choose and where it has come from.

Buying Second-hand

There are many outlets for purchasing a board second-hand. The most trusted way is via a surf shop, where they usually have a good selection on the rack that have been traded in. There is a wider selection available through online auction sites such as eBay and Gumtree. While there are more to choose from and you may bag a bargain, there are a number of things to avoid.

- Cracks – as mentioned, boards are comprised of a foam centre covered with a tough glass coat that protects the fragile core. Any cracks in the glass coat, whether on a PU board or an EPS, will allow water ingress, which

will lead to degradation of the foam. Small cracks can be fixed with a product such as Solarez (a tube of UV-curing resin that has strands of fibreglass running through it). It fills cracks and holes, then hardens to form a tough seal, allowing dings or punctures to be fixed in minutes.

- Dings – older boards may have little dents that have not actually punctured the surface. These are generally caused by day-to-day usage and the impact of knees or stones. A few on the deck are OK but there should not be too many on the underside of the board.

- Creases – these occur when a board has been hit by the lip of a wave with enough power to bend it. The telltale signs are a crease line or crack in the glass running around the bottom or

Rik 'Peg Leg Bennett dropping down a wave on his performance longboard. (Photo: Sarah Bunt)

top of the board. These boards should be avoided as the structural integrity has been compromised.

- Broken boards – these are sometimes repaired and put up for sale. Repairs can be seen as patches around the middle or areas where the board has been painted white to try to mask the repair job. While some repaired boards are structurally strong, the repair adds weight to the board and affects the way it rides. Also best avoided.

In general it is best for the inexperienced buyer to seek the advice of someone with good surfboard knowledge when buying second-hand.

Types of Surfboard

During the 1950s there was only one real surfboard design available and that was what we refer to today as the longboard or Malibu (although they weren't called longboards then). However, even in these early days there were maverick designers experimenting with board length, shape and fins. By the time the shortboard revolution came around the diversity of board styles had exploded. Today there is a dizzying array of craft to choose from, so the most important question to ask is: which will I have the most fun on?

Longboard

A longboard is designated as a board 9ft 1in in length or over for competition purposes, but unofficially is anything around or over the 9ft mark. They usually have a rounded nose and have either one or three fins. A traditional longboard, alternatively known as a Malibu, Mal, log or pig, is a thick, usually round-nosed board, with a lot of volume and a single fin, often glassed in. These boards are heavy and wide, often with an area of concave under the nose to help nose-riding. They are ridden in the traditional style, echoing the surfing of the 1950s and 1960s, with manoeuvres such as hang-tens, drop knee turns and cross stepping the board. Traditional logs are difficult to manoeuvre and impossible to duck dive. They are also extremely hard to ride in anything but small surf but provide a stable platform for walking up and down the board.

The second type is the progressive or performance longboard, a thinner, lighter craft, usually with three fins – either a thruster set-up or a two plus one. These boards are much more manoeuvrable, and are surfed in a modern dynamic style including vertical snaps, floaters and barrel riding. They can also be ridden in bigger surf – although are again virtually impossible for a human to duck dive, although I have seen it done!

Sean Lascelles walking to the nose on his traditional style longboard. (Photo: Sarah Bunt)

CHOOSING A SURFBOARD

Mini-mal

These boards share some of the characteristics of a longboard, in that they often have a rounded nose, are wider and thicker than a traditional shortboard and usually have a thruster fin set-up. Mini-mals can vary in length from between 6ft to about 8ft. Their balance of stability and manoeuvrability makes them a popular beginner to intermediate board.

Single Fin

The single fin was born out of the shortboard revolution that took place between 1967 and 1970. During this time visionaries such as Bob McTavish and George Greenough pioneered a change that saw average board sizes drop from 9ft 6in to 6ft 6in. Noses became pointed, boards became narrower and tails became pulled in to either a pin tail, rounded pin tail or diamond tail. The move to these shorter single fins precipitated a shift in surfing styles from manoeuvres taking place by the surfer on the board to the surfer manoeuvring the board on the wave.

Today there has been a rebirth of the traditional ethos of old school single fin surfing with the progressive single fin, an update on the classic but taking into account modern plan shapes, bottom contours and rails. These call for a very fluid style of surfing, linking turns and riding the high line, generating speed from the curl. Having a single fin in a quiver is a way to improve style and flow, as well as being versatile and great fun to ride.

Twin Fin

In 1977 Mark Richard rode a twinnie for the first time and it changed surfboard design forever. Modern twins benefit from decades of design tweaks such as

A surfer enjoying the small waves on his fish surfboard. (Photo: Sarah Bunt)

rails, bottom contours, tails, etc. The result is that some of the skitteriness has been lost, meaning modern twinnies offer a fast, fun, loose 'skatie' board that works well in 2–4ft clean surf.

Thruster

The thruster has dominated surfboard design for more than three decades. So dominant was Simon Anderson's 1981 three-fin design that for a long time many in surfing assumed that board design had reached its apex.

The classic thruster is a three-fin shortboard with a pointed nose. Traditionally ridden at a length anywhere between just under the corresponding height of the surfer, to 3in longer, this manoeuvrable board generates amazing drive through turns – hence the name for the 'thrust' it provides.

Many other design parameters go into a modern three-finned craft, incorporating numerous variations of length, width, nose, tail and rail and allowing the design to be tweaked to suit any kind of wave condition or standard of

surfing. The thruster is considered the most flexible board invented.

Quad

The quad is a four-fin design that has been around since the 1970s and was brought back to prominence by multiple world champion Kelly Slater, who liked the extra speed and grip it can provide in more hollow waves. Today, quad set-ups have become popular in shorter, wider designs that function well in smaller waves where extra speed is traded for a slight reduction in manoeuvrability or in longer, thinner craft to help lock into the wave face while barrel riding.

Fish

Fish are traditionally short, wide boards with pointed or rounded noses. They are characterized by the fact they have a wide swallow tail with twin fins or keels. Fish are great small wave boards; they catch waves easily and provide great down the line speed in weaker waves. However, they are harder to turn than conventional thrusters.

Mini-Simmons

Characterized by its short, stubby appearance, blunt or rounded nose and wide square tail, the Mini-Simmons takes its inspiration from the 1950s designs of California shaper Bob Simmons. The Mini-Simmons takes Bob's principles and whittles them down to ultra-short craft, usually between 4ft 10 in and 6ft. The boards have twin keel fins, the focus being to generate speed in smaller waves. They are also known as soap bars for their shape and 'slipperiness'. These boards are great fun to ride but much trickier for intermediate surfers than a standard shortboard.

Bonzer

Originally pioneered by the Campbell brothers (Malcolm and Duncan) in the early 1970s, the bonzer is a three-fin design that uses a large central single fin with two angled keel fins – scalene and right-angled in shape – with a number of deep rounded channels through the tail section.

Although years ahead of its time, the bonzer design never achieved widespread popularity. The Campbells further developed the design into a five-fin set-up. Combining the speed of a single fin with the manoeuvrability of the thruster, they have enjoyed a resurgence recently and received recognition for forging a design pathway missed by surfing's mainstream.

Gun (or Semi-Gun)

The term gun, or 'rhino chaser' refers to a board intended to paddle into and ride big waves. The characteristics of larger waves makes them harder to catch as they travel through the water at a greater velocity than smaller ones. Guns generally range from more than 7ft long anywhere up to nearly 10ft. This extra length and volume aids 'paddle-ability' in larger waves. They have a pointed nose with lots of nose rocker to aid steep drops, plus a drawn in pin tail to reduce drag and allow it to hang in steeper waves.

Mid-Length

The mid-length is usually a single fin board between 6ft 10in and 8ft, with a slightly pointed nose and narrower tail. These boards tend to follow a more traditional template from the early 1970s but often with a modern twist in rail and bottom contour to improve manoeuvrability while retaining the same flow. They are all about staying smooth, keeping in the most critical part of the wave, maintaining flow and trimming the high line.

Shortboard

The shortboard is traditionally under 6ft 6in with a three-fin thruster set-up, a pointed nose, gentle rocker and pulled in squash, round or pin tail. Today, shortboards are as diverse as you could imagine with any combination of length, nose, tail, rail and fin layout. Over the past few years board length has dropped to an extent that many surfboards are now 3 or 4in shorter, with the reduced length being replaced by a little more volume. Shortboards are not generally great for a beginner unless he or she is at the point where they are surfing out on the open face of the wave.

Leah Dawson with her five-finned bonzer.
(Photo: Kate Czuczman)

CHAPTER 5

OTHER EQUIPMENT

Grab a board, throw it in the back of a pick-up and bail for the beach – that's the surfing ideal. At first glance wave riding seems to be refreshingly clear of the clutter of kit and consumerism, however look more closely and there is a raft of surfing-related products competing for your well-earned pennies. Some are essential, some less so. One thing is certain, there'll always be a new gadget to covet.

Wetsuits

For surfers here in the UK a wetsuit is as important a purchase as a surfboard – in fact if you are a year round surfer you'll need two; one for winter and one for summer. Water temperatures around the British Isles do not allow the luxury of surfing without one, except for perhaps a couple of rare windless sunny days in August, so picking a good wetsuit is essential to make sure your surfing is warm, safe and enjoyable.

What is a Wetsuit?

A wetsuit is designed to keep a surfer warm in even the coldest of environments. It is not designed to do this by keeping the wearer dry – this is how a drysuit works but these are bulky and usually only worn by divers.

A wetsuit is made of a synthetic

An Xcel winter wetsuit with chest zip and built-in hood. (Photo: Xcel)

rubber-like material called neoprene. It acts primarily as an insulator, preventing heat loss. The suit also traps a very thin layer of water between the skin and the

wetsuit material. The body gives off heat that is lost through the skin. This thin neoprene envelope holds this heat, warming the water trapped next to the skin. If too much cold water is flushing into and around a wetsuit or if a wetsuit leaks, this leaches heat away and the surfer quickly becomes cold. This is the reason why the fit of a wetsuit is critical – too loose and water will flush through, causing heat loss.

What is Neoprene?

Neoprene is a flexible and durable synthetic rubber material. A wetsuit uses a foamed neoprene; that is a neoprene with a sponge-like consistency with 'pockets' filled with nitrogen gas. This makes the material a good insulator. As with many insulators, it is the air/gas in the substance that provides much of the insulation properties.

Neoprene is produced in huge sheets, and these are cut and attached together to produce an all-in-one suit. Panels of neoprene can be joined in a number of ways:

- Flatlock is basic stitching where the needle penetrates the two pieces of neoprene, pulling them together. Flatlock, however, allows some water seepage through the tiny holes created by the needle. This is acceptable on some summer suits where the water temperature is not too cold.

- Blind stitch is a method where the needle does not penetrate all the way through the neoprene, so there are no needle holes to allow water seepage. It is warmer but less durable than flatlock so is used in conjunction with glueing and taping of seams.
- Glue and taping sees panels glued together, with a strip of flexible tape bonded along the inside seam to add strength and make the join between the two pieces of neoprene waterproof.
- Fluid seams are a way of securing a panel without stitching, using a rubber-like glue to form a flexible and waterproof seam between panels, typical of top of the range wetsuits.

Kalani David, head to toe in neoprene. (Photo: Xcel)

Wetsuit Thickness

Wetsuits are graded by thickness, in millimetres, around the body and legs, for example a 5/3, 4/3 or 3/2. A standard summer suit is a 3/2, i.e. it has a 3mm of neoprene around the core of the body and 2mm around the arms and legs. A spring suit is usually a 4/3 and winter wetsuits are usually 5/4s.

Wetsuits are generally thicker around the body as this is the area that needs to be kept the warmest and thinner around the arms and legs as these are the parts that need to be given more flexibility for movement.

There are a number of wetsuit variations available on the market at the moment, so it is really a question of working out what is best for you and your surfing needs. For example, a surfer can select whether they want a wetsuit with long or short arms or legs for summer, or one with or without a built-in hood for winter. They can also choose to

go for an all-black wetsuit or one with pops of colour to set them apart from the crowd.

Suits are made from panels of either smooth skin/single-lined neoprene, or double-lined neoprene. Lining the neoprene with a flexible nylon material makes it more durable and less 'sticky', so it is easier to get in and out. Chest panels, back panels and hoods are mostly made of smooth skin/single-lined neoprene, as this loses less heat through evaporation, and therefore helps keep the core warmer in the wind.

Zips are major areas where water can seep into a wetsuit, and companies go to great lengths to develop mechanisms that keep water ingress to a minimum. Some wetsuits have a front zip, others have one on the back. These usually involve a flap of neoprene behind the zip. Zip technology is also an area companies are investing in, with new drylock style zips on offer in high-end winter suits.

With wetsuits fit is everything – you could invest in the best suit on the market but if it is the wrong size or a bad

fit for your body type you will either be cold or unable to move. Make sure you try on a number of wetsuits to get the best fit for you. Each manufacturer provides a size chart for height and weight. They should be snug without any bagginess. Particular areas to pay attention to are the small of the back and under arms. However, you should still be able to bend your knees and touch the ground unencumbered. If in doubt, buy from a reputable surf shop and ask for help from an assistant. They will be able to ensure you get the correct size.

Look After your Suit

There is one golden rule when it comes to looking after your wetsuit. Always rinse it out with fresh water when you've been in the sea or it will begin to smell and eventually it will deteriorate. A wetsuit that has been left wet with saltwater never totally dries out, and you may find that weeks later it is still wet inside. If your wettie begins to smell then wash it out in

Jimmy Pinfield opts for a long-legged, short-armed style. (Photo: Sarah Bunt)

a bucket using a small amount of very mild detergent and rinse it well. Never put your wetsuit in a washing machine! Also, try to avoid leaving it for too long in the sun as prolonged exposure to UV light degrades the neoprene. It is best to leave it to drip dry on a hanger out of the direct sunlight. Also, if you get any holes or tears, repair them quickly as small tears will grow and become harder to mend. You can do this with Black Witch, which is a tube of black rubber solution that glues damaged neoprene and can fix minor wetsuit damage.

Boots, Gloves and Hood

The odds are if you're going to surf all year round in the UK you'll need these – unless you are super hard core. Gloves and boots used to be cumbersome and inflexible items, often designed for divers or windsurfers. Today these accessories are made from super flexible neoprene and have decades of design poured into them. The results have transformed the winter surfing experience. Invest in a good set and you will forget you are wearing them. As with wetsuits, fit is everything – too small and they will cut

off your blood supply, too big and they will keep filling up with water or you will keep stubbing your toe when popping up.

Leashes

Prior to the 1970s surfers rode without leashes and if they lost their board during a wipe out they would have to swim to recover it. This had a number of drawbacks – a surfboard is an important buoyancy aid and if lost in big conditions it can leave a surfer in a potentially dangerous situation. Also, a lost board in

A leash doing its job by keeping the surfer attached to his board when he falls off. (Photo: Sarah Bunt)

the line-up can pinball around in the waves, wreaking havoc upon surfers on the inside. Plus, a lost board could easily end up lost in a rip or smashed on the rocks. Early leashes were pretty dangerous in that they were made from a length of elasticated bungee, which meant boards would often come pinging back at a surfer when he or she fell off. Today leashes are manufactured through a process that incorporates an elasticated core to allow stretch, surrounded by a less springy outer layer to prevent spring back. This results in a cord that stretches in a controlled manner without breaking or springing back.

Leashes attach via a nylon ankle strap, lined with neoprene to prevent rubbing, and secured with Velcro. There is a swivel between the strap and the cord to prevent the leash getting twisted. At the board end of the leash is another swivel, attached to a rail saver – a length of nylon strap designed to prevent the leash cutting into the board in the event of a heavy wipe out. The rail saver is tied to the leash plug of the board via a loop of strengthened nylon string.

Leashes are available in a number of lengths and thicknesses. Competition leashes tend to be thinner and lighter, big wave leashes tend to be thicker and longer, while longboard leashes are longer still.

Wax

The need for wax seems something of an anachronism in this modern age. The act of rubbing a coconut-scented block on to the deck of a computer-designed glossy stick is a throwback to the earliest days of wave riding. It's something that hasn't changed at all since the dawn of the Malibu era – as essential to the likes of Kelly Slater and Mick Fanning as it was to Mickey Dora and Mike Doyle.

Wax has one simple, yet essential, job – to provide traction for wet feet on a slippery surfboard deck. A board is a slick projectile, designed to glide with the least friction possible through the water. However, the surfer needs to be able to stand on the deck and this is where good old-fashioned wax come in. Originally paraffin wax (as used in candles) sufficed, but today there are a number of specially tailored blends on offer from a plethora of manufacturers. Cold water surf wax is softer and easier to apply on chilly winter days – but will melt too easily in warm conditions and leave a board slippery. Warm water surf wax is harder and resists melting but is difficult to apply in cold conditions.

When waxing a board, it is best to apply a base coat of hard wax first, followed by a top coat of the desired type. The hard base coat helps the top coat adhere better and makes the coat more durable. A wax comb can be useful if you have not got wax on hand as it reinvigorates a top coat of wax.

A block of cold water surf wax. (Photo: Ocean and Earth)

Traction Pads

During the 1980s deck grips/traction pads became popular. This large adhesive patch of textured foam sticks to the deck of the board to provide traction and was designed to replace wax. There were usually two – one placed near the tail of the board for the rear foot and one midway for the front foot. Early pioneers included brands such as Gorilla Grip and Astrodeck.

While the front pads gradually went out of fashion, the rear pads have remained relatively popular and are widely available, produced by brands and accessory companies including FCS, and Ocean and Earth. They are best applied to a board when new, before any wax has been applied – or a board must be cleaned meticulously to remove any traces of wax. They have a peel off adhesive surface on the reverse that sticks to the deck.

Today, tail pads can be split into two, three, four or five pieces, with a raised ridge at the back to prevent the foot slipping off. Fans of the rear deck pad claim it helps them to plant the rear foot in the right place, that the foam helps

protect the deck from pressure dings and that it provides better traction.

Sunblock

Good sun protection is an essential to protect exposed skin. The strength of the sun is magnified out in the water as the reflected rays from the surface of the water add to the amount of UV light to which the body is exposed. This means that even in the UK the sun will cause burning, while longer term exposure can increase the risk of conditions such as skin cancer. There are several good waterproof sunscreens and sunblocks on the market, including several products specially formulated for surfers.

Board Bags

If you've shelled out on your dream board, the last thing you want is for it to get damaged. Yet the likelihood is a surfboard is more likely to be damaged out of the water than in it. They get dropped, scraped, trodden on, placed on sharp objects and slammed by car boots – we have invented

a myriad of ways to accidentally damage our beloved sticks. And yet so many surfers seem reluctant to put their hands in their pockets for a board bag, even when they are an investment that will easily pay for themselves. Using one, your boards will last longer, are less likely to get damaged and are easier to handle. They also keep the board out of UV light, which causes it to become discoloured, degrades the strength of the resin and foam and generally makes it look old and uncared for.

Board bags come in many varieties:

- Board socks – These are old-school elasticated socks with a drawstring offer a small degree of protection
- Day bags – These lightweight, padded zip-up bags are often a reflective silver to cut down on heat when left in a car on a sunny day. These are a good basic bag for use around home breaks or on trips in a car
- Travel bags – These have thicker padding, more durable with room for extra paddling such as bubble wrap and foam. They come in various lengths and some offer room for two or three boards. Designed for the rigours of airline travel
- Coffins – These are substantial bags for multiple boards, durable and robust – often with wheels for ease of transport. Essential kit for a travelling professional surfer.

We have all heard stories of airline baggage handlers who have 'accidentally' dropped the boards of visiting surfers. So it is best to invest in the best bag you can afford as well as learning how to wrap it well for travelling. Get saving that bubble wrap and invest in some foam pipe lagging.

A three-piece tail pad. (Photo: Ocean and Earth)

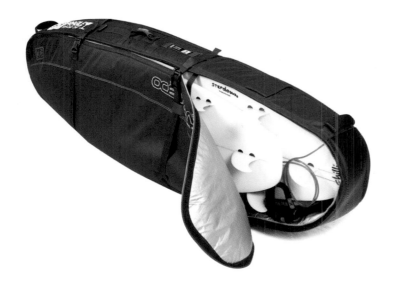

A coffin bag for carrying multiple boards. (Photo: Ocean and Earth)

Rash Vests

Rash vests are either short sleeve or long sleeve Lycra tops with high necks. They were traditionally worn to prevent wetsuits from rubbing in areas such as under arms and around necks. Wetsuits used to be pretty inflexible and the neoprene could be stiff. Today, with modern wetsuit technology there is no need for rash vests – suits are soft and a good brand should not rub.

Rashies also became popular for tropical waters to prevent wax rash when surfing without a wetsuit. However, with the increasing awareness of the dangers of exposure to the sun, rash vests have become important tools in preventing sunburn and UV exposure. Many brands of rash vests now have inbuilt UV protection for those midday sessions in places such as Indonesia, Australia or Central America.

Earplugs

If you plan to surf a lot, especially in cold water, then you'll need to start looking after your ears. Cold water flushing and wind whistling in your ears leads to a condition known as exostosis or surfer's ear. This is where the cold water stimulates abnormal bone growth within the ear, causing the bone of the ear canal to thicken. This in turn leads to a narrowing of the ear canal, which can trap water and wax in the ear and lead to infections. In severe cases the ear canal can close altogether. The only cure for surfer's ear is an operation to drill or chisel away the bone. Prevention is the best route and the best way to avoid surfer's ear is by wearing custom-made earplugs that fit into the ear and prevent water ingress. A good alternative are the silicon plugs available through your local surf shop or pharmacy. The more often a person surfs and the colder the environment, the quicker the rate of bone growth. According to the California Ear Institute, cold water surfers experience exostosis at a rate 600 per cent higher than warm water surfers.

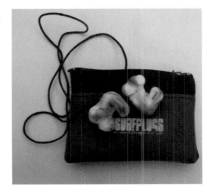

Earplugs, essential for the cold water surfer. (Photo: Approaching Lines)

Key Locks

The conundrum of what to do with your car keys when going for a surf used to be easily solved; most wetsuits had and still have key pockets built in. However, modern keys have evolved into bulky items with complex internal electrical circuits that cannot get wet. Hence the invention of the surf key lock. These are small boxes into which keys are placed, attached through the tow loop to the car and secured by a combination lock. N.B. the wheel arch of your car, while seemingly convenient, is not a secure place to stash your key!

The Bucket

A solution to the problem of how to store a soaking wetsuit without

The humble but very useful bucket. (Photo: Approaching Lines)

drenching the back of your car is the humble builder's bucket! Readily available from your local DIY store, it has long since become an essential piece of surfer's kit. These brightly coloured tubs are big enough to stand in while getting changed out of your wettie in a muddy car park, and also have enough room to store wetsuits, boots, gloves, towels, etc. Plus, you can wash out your suit in it when you get home.

Spare Fins

Modern fins are designed to snap off on impact without damaging the board, so

The invaluable fin key. (Photo: Approaching Lines)

be sure to have a spare set in case of a mishap on the best day of the year. Fins are available in a huge variety of sizes and shapes and it pays to experiment with different set-ups in varying conditions. For example, use a slightly bigger set of fins to help bite and drive when the surf is big and a smaller set to reduce drag in lesser waves.

Fin Key

This is the invaluable tool that enables a surfer to take the fins in and out of his or her board. This hexagonal key is universal and essential kit. Be sure to put them somewhere safe – they have a nasty habit of disappearing just when you need them! You may need to replace them from time to time as they have a tendency to round off and stop working if used frequently.

Snacks and Drinks

It is always underestimated how essential it is to stay hydrated, especially when staying in the water for long surf sessions. Drink plenty of water before and after surfing. Many brands now offer stainless steel bottles as an alternative to plastic bottled water. Refill from the tap and reuse for a lifetime – better for your wallet and the environment.

A banana gets you out of a tight spot and can be the difference between a second surf or not. Any fruit or an energy bar make great surf snacks and help give you that extra bit of paddle power or can help raise your energy levels for the drive home after an epic session!

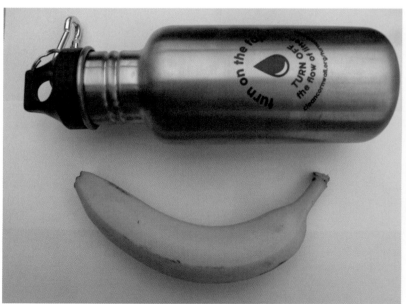

Water and a banana, the perfect pre-surf fuel. (Photo: Approaching Lines)

CHAPTER 6

LOOKING AFTER YOUR SURFBOARD

Although surfboards have a degree of strength and resilience, they can also be quite fragile and are susceptible to particular types of damage. Dings in the glass coat are easily picked up by placing the board bottom side down on the ground and cracks can appear on the rail from the most innocuous of knocks.

It is a good idea to invest in a good board bag to prevent those little knocks and dings from the back of the car or van. A board bag will also shade a board from the damaging UV rays that will discolour and degrade a board, eventually turning it from white to a 'biscuity' brown.

It is a good idea to clean off the old wax on the deck of a board regularly.

Wax builds up into a thick layer and will lead to more pressure dings on the deck of the board. Leave the board in the sun for a short while to soften the wax before using a scraper on your wax comb to remove it. Then reapply a fresh coat, using a harder base coat first, followed by a suitable top coat of either warm water, cool water or cold water wax.

Wax combs are plastic and have a serrated edge to comb the surface wax and freshen it up, and a straight edge for cleaning off wax. Ensure the bottom of the board is wax free, using the scraper.

Packing your Bag

A good board bag comes with a degree of protection for the surfboard. It will have inbuilt padding to help cushion minor knocks associated with day-to-day handling and moving a board in and out of a car or van. Packing needs a little more thought when it comes to travelling abroad by plane. Here your precious surfboard will be handed over to baggage handlers to be packed in a hold along with many heavy and sharp items of luggage.

Pack Light

There is one school of thought that believes in keeping a board bag light by not adding any extra protection. The

Wax combs are essential for removing old surf wax before applying a new coat. (Photo: Ocean and Earth)

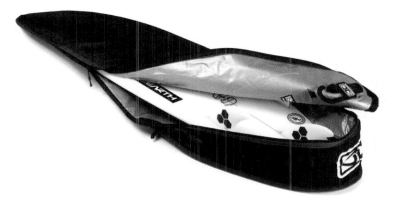

A lightly packed board is easier to carry. (Photo: Ocean and Earth)

theory is that it makes the bag easier to handle and therefore less likely to suffer the bangs and bumps that damage boards.

Pack Substantially

The other school of thought is to wrap up the board with as much padding as possible. Unfortunately not all baggage handlers are as careful as one would hope, so it does pay to add a little extra protection. A badly damaged board can ruin a long saved for surf trip.

The first thing is to protect the rails, nose and tail as these are the areas most at risk. The best protection is pipe lagging, the long tubular foam insulation available from most DIY stores. This foam has a slit cut into it longitudinally so that the tube can be opened out into a C shape in cross section. Push the lagging on to the

A typical kit that you would need for repairing small dings on your board. (Photo: Ocean and Earth)

rail, running from nose to tail and secure with tape. Repeat for the other side.

Bubble wrap can then be layered across the deck and the underside of the board to provide an additional barrier. You can also use items that you are taking

on the trip such as wetsuits and towels to provide even more protection.

Ding Repair

For the inevitable, always take a good ding repair kit on a surf trip! Unfortunately it is not uncommon for boards to be damaged in transit. Solarez is a great way to fix dings and will provide a watertight fix in minutes for small punctures or cracks. (It is also worth having a small piece of cling film and some very fine sandpaper with you to aid the job!) Another method that may help in a tight spot is duct tape; strong waterproof tape that can adhere to a cracked nose or tail to provide a temporary fix for a short trip. Many surf destinations also have a local 'ding repair guy' who can fix boards and get them back to you quickly for a reasonable price. It pays to ask around.

CHAPTER 7

WEATHER, SWELL AND WAVES

As surfers we are all obsessed with the weather forecast. What will conditions be like over the next week, from which direction will the wind blow and how strong? But why is all this so important?

Where do Waves Come From?

A wave is a form of energy moving through the ocean as a series of peaks and troughs. A wave that breaks on a particular beach, say Fistral in Cornwall, could have been birthed in a hurricane off the coast of the West Indies, or in a low pressure system formed over Canada or Greenland. Waves can travel thousands of miles across open ocean and take days to arrive at a shoreline. A good meteorologist can learn how to predict when a swell will arrive at a surf break and be there to meet it. In the big wave community it is not unusual for these surfers, guys such as Garrett McNamara, Greg Long and Andrew Cotton, to have bags ready to leave for the other side of the globe on a promising chart. Such surfers are driven by the desire to score the largest waves ever ridden at some of the world's big wave hotspots. However, these trips can often end up being in vain as charts can suddenly change, resulting in the swell not delivering the required size of surf.

It all comes down to understanding how our planet's weather systems work.

Robin Kent on a good size wave caused by a low pressure system out to sea. (Photo: Sarah Bunt)

Low Pressure System

A low pressure system is also known as a depression or a cyclone. The sun's energy warms a region of the earth's surface. Air is heated by the land and rises. However, there is an uneven heating of the surface. In an area of low pressure, warmer air is rising as it is less dense. As it rises, it leaves behind an area of low pressure, drawing in air from the surrounding regions to take its place.

The air travelling into a low pressure system does not travel in a straight line, it is drawn into an ever decreasing spiral. This is caused by the rotation of the earth. In the Northern Hemisphere, air spirals into a low pressure system in an anticlockwise direction – however in the Southern Hemisphere it is drawn in a clockwise direction. This is known as the Coriolis effect.

Air rising in a low pressure system cools as it ascends, and the water vapour it carries condenses into clouds and rain. This is why a low pressure system tends to bring unsettled weather and rain with it

High Pressure System

An area of high pressure or an anticyclone, is a region where the air is

41

denser and is therefore falling, creating a greater relative pressure at the surface. Air moves out of a high pressure system in a clockwise spiral in the Northern Hemisphere and an anticlockwise direction in the Southern Hemisphere.

A high pressure system has air descending that tends to have already lost its water vapour, meaning these systems bring clear skies and settled weather.

Wind

The pressure difference within the atmosphere causes air to be drawn into the low pressure area from the high pressure area. We can feel this moving air as wind. A deep low rolling across the Atlantic can generate strong storm force winds as it draws air in. Really deep depressions are known as hurricanes or cyclones.

It is possible to map the pressure at the earth's surface using barometers. Points of the same pressure can be joined on a map by lines known as isobars. These isobars help map the size and scale of pressure systems and the direction and strength of winds. Where isobars are far apart there is a very gradual pressure difference or pressure gradient, so winds are light. Where isobars are very close together there is a steep pressure gradient and so winds will be very strong.

This relates to wave formation as it is the wind blowing across the surface of the ocean that generates waves. The stronger the wind, the longer the wind blows and the greater the distance or fetch over which the wind blows, the bigger the waves will be.

Fetch

The distance over which the wind blows not only affects the size of waves generated, it also affects the wave period; that is the distance between each wave. A short period means the waves are close together, meaning a less powerful swell. The greater the period, the longer the time between each wave and the cleaner and more powerful the swell.

Swells

At the centre of the low pressure storm cell, the sea tends to be stormy, peaky and confused. But as the waves travel away from the storm that birthed them, they become organized into rolling waves. Close to the depression the rolling waves are known as a windswell. A windswell has waves that are very close together and these tend to be weak and choppy and lacking in power.

As the swell moves away from the low pressure it becomes more organized and forms what is known as a groundswell. In a groundswell, waves travel in sets of six or seven larger waves moving at the same speed. Set waves arrive on the beach and are bigger and more powerful than the other waves in between.

Surfers look for a number of things when they study the weather: a low pressure that is 'deep' enough to generate strong winds (usually below 996mb), far enough away to smooth it into a good groundswell (two to three days) and one that will blow long enough

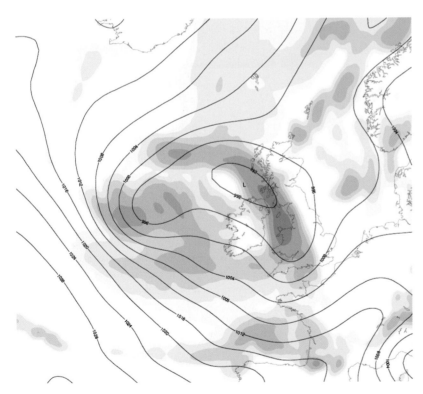

A pressure chart showing a low pressure system of 992mb. The closer the isobars are together, the stronger the wind. (Photo: MagicSeaweed)

to create good conditions for a few days. Surfers will get to know where on the weather map the low pressure needs to be in order to produce the best waves for their local surfing area.

Why do Waves Break?

A good groundswell travelling through the open ocean can be almost invisible in deep water. Once it reaches shallower waters the swell lines become more visible – they have a look of advancing corduroy.

As the wave runs into shallow water it begins to 'feel' the bottom, the energy becomes more compressed and the wave begins to rise in height. As the water becomes shallower the friction from the bottom causes the wave to rise further and the bottom of the wave slows in comparison with the top, causing the wave to spill forward and break.

The bottom contour of the beach or reef affects the way a wave breaks. A long slow decrease in depth will lead to weaker spilling waves, a sudden decrease in depth will cause a wave to pitch into a more powerful hollow shape. An example is the waves of Hawaii and Tahiti, which are powerful as they arrive from very deep water and break suddenly on to shallow reefs. In contrast, the waves in Holland travel through the shallow North Sea, which causes them to lose energy before eventually breaking.

How do Local Conditions Affect Waves?

A wave that leaves the warm equatorial waters may arrive thousands of miles away in local conditions that have a huge impact on wave quality. While swell size is

determined by wind strength and fetch, wave quality is affected by a number of factors. We have seen how the bottom contour of the beach or reef can affect how a wave breaks but it can also be affected by factors such as local wind strength, local wind direction, state of tide and coastal contours.

Local Wind

The local weather will have a huge impact on wave quality. For optimum wave quality a lack of wind will lead to glassy conditions, which means the waves will be clean with very few bumps and chop on the face. An offshore – that is a wind that blows from the land out to sea – is most beneficial for wave quality. It helps ensure a wave has more pitch, it grooms the waves – meaning they have clean faces – and can turn spilling waves into pitching waves. Light offshores ensure good wave quality, however if the offshores are too strong then they can begin to have a detrimental effect. They make it harder to paddle into waves, obscure the surfer's view due to the spray generated and can even begin to start blowing the surf flat.

Onshore wind – that is wind that blows from the sea on to the land – is less helpful for a surfer as it makes the waves more choppy and bumpy by causing them to crumble sooner. It can transform a lined up ordered swell into a bumpy and confused sea.

Tides

The gravitational pull of the moon circling the earth causes the ocean to be pulled towards it. You can see this locally as the tidal flow. When the moon is on the far side of the world, it will be low tide here.

In the UK the sea moves in and out twice in a twenty-four-hour period. The state of tide will have an impact at most breaks, as will whether a tide is dropping or pushing in. Some breaks only work on a low tide while others work only at high tide. Also, a pushing tide can give a small swell a bit more size, while a dropping tide may see a small swell diminish in size. Be aware that tides can also affect the access to and from a break as well as the amount of each that is visible. Tides change daily – not just the times of high and low tides but also the height of the tide. Operating on a monthly lunar cycle, the smallest tides are called neaps and the largest tides are called spring tides. Tides at beaches around the coastline will also be different so it is important to check the tide times of the break you are surfing.

Coastal Contours

When a wave reaches shallow water and begins to break, the shape of the seabed will have a huge impact on the size and shape of the wave, as well as the length of the wall – and hence the length of ride – a wave produces. As tides and swells move the ocean around, sandbanks are deposited and groomed. A sandbar at a beach may be laid down in a straight line so that a wave breaks as a close-out; that is the whole length of the wave breaks at once. However, if a sandbar has the correct angle, a wave may pitch and break at one end and peel along the sandbar, producing a long wall – and hence a long ride. Sandbars change over time and once excellent breaks can become close-outs, and vice versa. There are a number of famous beach breaks that produce consistent high quality banks due to the local geographical and oceanographic conditions. These include Supertubes in Portugal, Graviere in

Joel Gray on a right-hander. (Photo: Sarah Bunt)

Say this fast and it will confuse everyone, but a regular footer will ride a right, facing the wave and a goofy footer will ride it backhand. A left is ridden by a regular footer on his or her backhand and a goofy footer will be riding it forehand and facing the wave.

How to Check the Surf

The more you surf, the more you can see how different conditions affect different spots. You can also try your hand at forecasting when the waves will be good, using weather maps with low pressures and isobars marked on. But if you haven't mastered the finer points of swell prediction, don't worry. There are plenty of other ways to find out if the swell has arrived or is on its way.

Internet webcams have become a valuable resource for predicting when a swell is going to hit and checking if a swell has arrived. There are a couple of great sites such as MagicSeaweed.com that are incredible resources, offering swell predictions for all parts of the world. These sites will give you all the information that you need including predicted wave size, wind and swell direction and the tide times for different areas.

France, Black's in California and Puerto Escondido in Mexico.

Another way that high quality sandbanks can be produced is where a river meets the sea. Here sand may be deposited in a long curving bar perfect for peeling waves. Famous river mouths include Mundaka in Spain or Torrisdale in Scotland.

A reef is a solid platform upon which waves break. Due to the fact they are made of a hard substance such as rock, coral or boulder, a reef is permanent and does not shift. They are more consistent and should provide similar waves in similar conditions. Some reefs are angled in such a way that they produce world class waves when a swell arrives. They are still affected by wind, tide and swell direction, but as the platform always has the same shape it is more dependable. Famous reef breaks include Pipeline in Hawaii, Lance's Right in Indonesia and Thurso East in Scotland.

A point break is a wave that peels down the side of a headland, spit or peninsula. When a swell arrives from deep water and hits an area of land that is angled to the sea, it may pitch and break, producing long waves that peel along the point. These may be sand bottomed, coral reefs, rock platforms or boulders. Point breaks produce some of the longest waves in the world. These include the sand bottomed waves at Chicama in Peru, Skeleton Bay in Namibia or the Superbank in Australia. There are also reef points such as Sunset in Hawaii, Coxos in Portugal or G-Land in Indonesia plus boulder points including Rincon or Porlákshöfn in Iceland.

Peaks, Lefts and Rights

One thing that confuses non-surfers and beginners alike is whether a wave is peeling right or left. It might look like it should be a left, but in fact it is a right. Why? The direction of a wave is decided not by the way the wave peels when looked at from the shore, but from the way the wave is peeling when you are riding it. So a wave you go right on is a right-hander, and when watched from the beach it will seem to be peeling left.

Wave Size

Measuring wave size is difficult. In general surf parlance, swell size and wave size are two different things. A 2ft swell may break producing a 2ft wave, but at another spot the bottom contours may mean the wave face produced is 3ft. Also, a 1ft wave is not technically 1ft high – it would be more like knee high. A 2ft wave would be waist high, 3ft shoulder high

Kai Thomas on a left-hander. (Photo: Sarah Bunt)

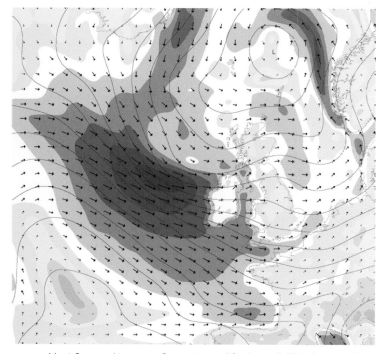

MagicSeaweed is a great forecasting tool for the surfer. This chart combines isobars or pressure and wind strength. The darker the colour, the stronger the wind on the Beaufort scale. (Photo: MagicSeaweed)

and 4ft head high or just over. This is a subjective measurement used by surfers and in no way scientific. If one were to say they rode a 6ft wave, it would not be head high on a 6ft person – probably closer to one and a half to twice their height – a 10 to 12ft face.

The only scientific measurement comes into measuring a wave when it is being considered as an entrant into the annual WSL Big Wave Awards, which judges the biggest waves surfed and caught on camera that year. Here the height of the surfer is taken and the wave height extrapolated from that. It is then possible to judge just how high was the biggest wave ridden.

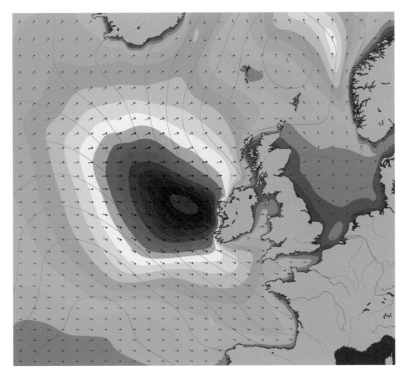

This MagicSeaweed chart shows the swell generated by the low pressure system. Again, the darker the colour, the bigger the swell. It's going to be a massive day in Ireland and a great day for the south-west. (Photo: MagicSeaweed)

Ben Skinner coping extremely well with strong offshore conditions. (Photo: Sarah Bunt)

CHAPTER 8

THE RULES OF SURFING

Over the years surfing has developed an etiquette – a set of rules that have evolved to help keep the line-up safe and to stop the assembled assortment of surfers of all ages and abilities descending into total anarchy. If you stick to surfing's commandments, and remember to treat the ocean, surfing and fellow surfers with respect, you should be fine. There are an increasing number of surfers in the water year on year so it is becoming more important to stick to these 'rules' in order to make your session a good one. Remember, it is supposed to be fun!

A surfer 'dropping in' on another surfer's wave. (Photo: Sarah Bunt)

Rules are essential in surfing to avoid scenes such as this. (Photo: Sarah Bunt)

Don't Drop in

Never take off on a wave that another surfer, who is closer to the curl, is already riding on. This is the number one rule in surfing.

It can be tempting to try and paddle for every wave – especially on a busy day, but there are enough waves for everyone and sometimes you will have to be patient for your turn. Always use your eyes and ears to check if someone is already up and riding. If they are, let them enjoy it, it'll be your turn soon. Dropping in isn't just annoying; it can be dangerous, too. Taking off on a wave that is being ridden often results in surfers colliding, which risks them causing damage to each other and/or their surfboards.

Priority

The surfer nearest to the curl always has priority to go.

The part of the wave closest to the breaking section is the steepest and most powerful. This makes it the hardest place to take off. The surfer who takes off closest to the curl has priority. These tend

It is important to avoid surfers riding a wave when paddling out. (Photo: Sarah Bunt)

Beginner surfers staying on 'the inside' while an expert is 'out the back'. (Photo: Sarah Bunt)

to be the better surfers or the locals who know the break well. If you're learning you can pick up some smaller waves on the 'inside' as you work your way up the pecking order.

Paddling out

Be careful not to get in the way of a surfer who's up and riding while you are paddling out.

At point and reef breaks use the channels to get out and at beach breaks always keep your eyes open. If a surfer is riding, paddle out of the way and aim to paddle behind the surfer into the whitewater and not on to the face and into their path. The onus is on the surfer paddling out to try to ensure they are not in the path of a surfer that is up and riding.

Beginners Stay Inside

Just because you see a busy line-up out the back doesn't mean that is where you should be learning.

If you are not yet proficient in catching waves stick to the whitewater on the inside until you have mastered the basic skills. Then try a beginner-friendly break where the waves roll and are easier to catch.

Snaking

Never try to paddle round a surfer who is already paddling for a wave in an attempt to get closer to the peak and steal their wave.

This is the kind of thing that really gets people riled. Be patient and wait for the next wave.

Wave Hogs

Don't steal all the waves, especially if you are visiting a new break for the first time.

Nobody likes a wave hog. Just because you can catch all the waves doesn't mean you should. This is especially true of SUPs and longboards, which have the ability to get on to waves further out the back. This will win you few friends, so share the waves and create a good vibe in the water.

Bailing

Never bail your board and let it fly out behind you.

If a wave is heading your way and you have not mastered duck diving, try to keep a tight hold and roll over. If you are in this situation, take a look around to make sure no one is paddling close by. If there are surfers behind you, you must keep hold of it. Bear in mind that your board may be 6 or 7ft long, your leash the same – that means if you let go it could hit someone who is as far as 15ft behind you. You won't make friends by introducing them to the sharp end of your board!

Leave Nothing on the Beach but Footprints

Make sure you take home all your litter. It only takes a few minutes to pick up any pieces of plastic, wrappers or cans that have washed up and drop them in the bin on your way up the beach. It's good Karma and helps keep the beach clean.

Right: It is easy to get caught out when the waves pick up quickly. (Photo: Sarah Bunt)

PART II

TECHNICAL SKILLS

CHAPTER 9

READING THE OCEAN

Surfers assessing the conditions before heading out for a surf. (Photo: Kate Czuczman)

Surfers walking along the beach at low tide. (Photo: Sarah Bunt)

It's important to realize that the coastline is an ever-changing canvas. Conditions can switch quickly, swell sizes can increase and tides can push in, causing a once large beach to disappear. It is important to be aware of your surroundings as well as forewarned about potential dangers.

What is the Swell Forecast?

A small friendly benign day in the water can change quickly if a huge long period swell arrives suddenly. Be sure to check the forecast on a reliable website such as MagicSeaweed.com so you are aware of what your surf has in store. If you are still finding your feet as a surfer, best to stick to a safer lifeguarded beach.

Know the Tides

Some beaches are huge open areas of sands with easy access at all tides. Others appear large at low tide, but when the tide pushes in, the sea may completely cover the beach. This can be a real problem if the sand is backed by cliffs. Every year people are cut off in bays that seemed safe at low tide, only for the access points to completely disappear as the tide pushed in. If in doubt, ask a lifeguard. Many guarded beaches have tide times posted as well as maps warning of potential dangers. If in doubt,

Lifeguards are always aware of any rips and currents. (Photo: Sarah Bunt)

stick to a lifeguarded beach.

Rips and Currents

As a wave breaks on to a sandbar or reef, the sea spills forward as whitewater surging up the beach. It then drains away back into deeper water. The water heading back out to sea usually runs through deeper channels between sandbanks, causing currents known as riptides or rips. Standing on the beach you will notice areas where the waves break forming whitewater and areas where no waves are breaking. The channels with no whitewater are usually where rip currents form. Rips can travel surprisingly quickly pulling a swimmer out to sea before they realize they are in trouble.

As a surfer there are a number of things to take into account when entering the water. Always be aware of your position, both in relation to how far down the beach you are and how far out you are. This is easily done by picking your line-up and triangulating your position in relation to a number of prominent features on land. For example a telegraph pole, a house or a rocky peak. If you have a telegraph pole lined up with a house and you find the pole has moved, it is not the pole that has changed position but you.

If a surfer becomes caught in a rip current it is very difficult to paddle directly against the direction of flow. A surfer fighting a rip will soon become exhausted. To escape a rip one must paddle across the flow, either up or down the beach, where the rip can be exited easiest. Once out of the rip it is then possible to either paddle in or catch a wave in.

If you are an inexperienced surfer ask the lifeguards and they will point out where potentially dangerous currents are and where to avoid

Other Potential Hazards

Weever fish are only small, perhaps the size of a little finger. They spend their time buried in the sand in the warm shallows, especially at low tide. They are protected by a dorsal spine and are mildly venomous. If stepped on they inject the venom into the foot, the pain being on a par with a bee or wasp sting. Treatment should be administered immediately by immersing the foot into very hot water, being careful not to burn the skin. The heat from the water breaks down the protein in the venom and the foot should be immersed for about thirty minutes.

Most RNLI lifeguard huts have a facility set up to treat weever stings.

Jellyfish are present in UK waters and are particularly prevalent after a period of onshore winds. There are six species commonly found around the UK and, although most do sting, they are relatively harmless. Occasionally the Portuguese man o' war (a jellyfish-like organism) and other more exotic species drift into UK waters. These stings can be quite painful. To treat them, remove tentacles from the skin. Affected areas should be washed with fresh water, not vinegar, alcohol or urine. Seek immediate medical assistance if a person experiences severe, lasting pain, or if the affected area becomes infected.

Rocks or Submerged Hazards

A surfer needs to be aware of the ever-changing line-up as tides push in and out. As the depth of water changes, rocks and other objects (for example, groynes) once hidden beneath the waves can become shallow enough to offer a potential hazard to the surfer. Be aware of 'boils' and disturbances in the water and keep your eyes open for rocks in the shallows. Even a beach that appears to be a huge stretch of sand can hide rocky outcrops as the tide recedes. When in doubt, ask.

Experienced surfers avoiding the rocks. (Photo: Sarah Bunt)

CHAPTER 10

CATCHING THE WHITEWATER

Surfing is one of the hardest things to learn. With snowboarding, mastering the basics may take someone with a good sense of balance a few days – in surfing you can multiply that by weeks, possibly months. Yet it is also one of the most rewarding and addictive things to do. Be prepared – it can change your life.

For those entering the water for the first time the advice would always be find a good surf school or coach and commit to a few lessons to help get you started. This will help with the basics such as water safety, equipment and technique, plus you'll be together with other learners making the whole experience more fun. Ask around or check online for one with a good reputation.

A young surfer enjoying a whitewater wave. (Photo: Sarah Bunt)

Board

Start with a 'foamie' – a foam board available to rent from most surf shops and hires. These boards are light and easy to handle and being foam it means you won't get injured if the board hits you in the turbulent whitewater.

Goofy or Regular?

The first step is to determine if you are a goofy footer or a regular footer. A goofy footer will stand on a surfboard with their right foot forward and their left foot on the tail, and a regular footer will do

A regular footer. (Photo: Sarah Bunt)

A goofy footer. (Photo: Sarah Bunt)

the opposite.

To determine if you are regular or goofy, stand with your feet shoulder width apart on the beach. Have a friend stand behind you and get them (without warning) to give you a gentle nudge in the middle of the back, pushing you forward. The foot you put forward first to break your fall is the foot that will be your front foot when surfing. It is important to get this right as it will make your surfing journey a lot easier. Don't just assume you are a regular footer.

Practise your paddling on the sand before entering the water. (Photo: Approaching Lines)

Leash

The leash will attach you to your surfboard and prevent it being washed away when you fall off. And you fall off a lot when learning. It attaches around your ankle via a Velcro and neoprene fastener. Attach the leash to your trailing ankle; that is the foot that is placed at the back of your board. On a goofy footer that will be the left, on a regular footer the right.

On the Sand

There are a few a few things to practise before hitting the water. The first is where to lie on your board. Lie on the deck with your centre of gravity over the centre line, or 'stringer'. Move forwards and backwards until you feel that the board is lying flat and balanced. The aim is that the nose of the board will not be under the water or sticking up in the air. Lift your head, arching your back so you are looking straight ahead, and paddle one arm at a time as if you are doing the crawl. You need to do this smoothly, keeping as close to the centre line as possible to keep the board stable and to stop it rocking wildly from side to side. Remember, the idea is to glide. As with everything in surfing, even this is harder than it sounds.

The Pop

'Popping up' is when you go from lying to standing on your board. The idea is that you pop to your feet in one fluid movement, as opposed to scrambling to an eventually upright position.

To pop up, as with paddling, lie on your stomach in the middle of your board, with your feet over the fins. Place the palms of your hands on your board

The pop step 1. (Photo: Approaching Lines)

The pop step 2. (Photo: Approaching Lines)

The pop step 3. (Photo: Approaching Lines)

The pop step 4. (Photo: Approaching Lines)

under your shoulders. Arch your back, keeping your head up and push your body up as if you are going to do a press-up. At the same time bring your front foot forward and under your stomach. Push down with your front foot, making your body rise until you are standing in a crouched position with your bum in, shoulders square to the board, facing forward. Your back foot should be over the fins, placed flat and horizontal to the board while your front foot should be in the middle of the board, again placed flat at a 45 degree angle to your back foot.

It is hard at first but the idea is that you do this all in one fluid motion! If you try to stand up straight, you'll just fall off again so you need to keep your centre of gravity low and your knees bent. This is harder to master than it looks, even on the beach.

Catching the Whitewater

The next step is to venture into the whitewater and catch a wave. The idea is not to try to stand up yet – but to ride a wave prone, i.e. lying down.

Wade out to waist deep, place the board facing the beach and lie on the deck in the paddle position, facing the beach. Look over your shoulder and as you see the whitewater approaching, begin paddling towards the beach, making sure your path is free from other surfers and water users. The idea is that you are travelling at the same speed as the wave by the time it reaches you. If not it will simply break over you, generally catapulting you off your board. As the whitewater picks you up, you will feel yourself accelerate forward. Try this a few times until you get to grips with how it feels and ultimately get the knack of paddling for and catching waves.

Popping Up in the Whitewater

This time, as the wave picks you up and you feel the board begin to accelerate, stop paddling and try to pop to your feet. This is much harder than it is on the beach. The board no longer has the support of the sand to keep it stable, so if you are slightly off balance you will find yourself in the drink. Don't worry about falling off – a fact of surfing life is that everyone does. One thing to remember is not to dive off head first – the water you're learning in is pretty shallow.

The next step to master is that once you're upright, stay low and balanced, keep your arms tucked and pointed forward. Look at the beach, stay focused. The key to surfing is repetition. Keep practising.

It is important to stay low and balanced once you've popped to your feet. (Photo: Sarah Bunt)

CHAPTER 11

ON TO THE GREEN

This is about taking what you've learned in the whitewater out on to unbroken waves. Pick a very small day at first, in a beginner-friendly location. The first step is more about judging when a wave is going to break and trying to catch that unbroken wave rather than the whitewater.

Catching Unbroken Waves

For this you need to understand a bit about waves and how they work. As a wave approaches the beach, the water gets gradually shallower, which causes the waves to steepen and eventually break. If you sit for a while and watch surfers, you will see that the best place to be when catching a wave is next to the 'curl' – near the part of the wave that is actually breaking. This is because it is the steepest part of the wave and will help to propel you on to the open face.

Having watched from the beach, paddle out to the line-up, sitting just behind where the bigger waves or 'set waves' are breaking. Sit and watch as a few sets come through so you can judge where and when the waves break – the bigger waves will break further out and the smaller ones closer in. You can also pick up tips just by watching other surfers in the water.

Paddling into Green Waves and Going Straight

The trick to progressing on to the face is to judge when a wave will break. If you pop too early the wave will not be steep enough and will leave you behind. If you pop too late the wave will have broken and turned into whitewater and it will be impossible to get from there on to the green face.

Lie on the board facing the beach and as the wave approaches begin to paddle harder – you need to be travelling at a speed similar to the wave. As the wave steepens the face will pick you up and

begin to push you forward. Once you feel this acceleration, pop to your feet and remain low, knees bent.

Paddling into Green Waves and Riding on to the Face

Once you have caught a few green waves and feel you are getting the hang of when a wave will break and where to be, it is time to try getting out on to the green, open face. The first step is to check which way the wave is breaking. It will be breaking either to the left or right. There are two ways to get on to the face. The first is to paddle straight, feel the wave

A surfer on a foamie riding the green face of the wave. (Photo: Sarah Bunt)

begin to push and pop to your feet. Then gently put pressure on to the side of the board in the direction you'd like to travel, so either the toe edge or the heel edge. This will cause the board to turn in that direction as the rail begins to bite into the water. Try and keep this subtle to start with.

Another method is to slightly angle your board in the direction you want to travel in – either left or right. When you feel the wave pick up your board and begin to carry you forward, pop to your feet. As your board is angled, it should be moving out on to the open face – if not, lean gently into the wave.

Once you have moved on to the unbroken part of the wave you will feel the real power of the wave as the steep, curling part of the face is the fastest place to ride. Your board should be angled to run across the wave – this is called trimming.

The Duck Dive

There is one major obstacle between the whitewater shallows and being able to get out the back to where the unbroken green waves are – and that is the breaking waves themselves. On a small day it is possible to wait for a lull in the waves and paddle out between the sets. However, when the waves pick up in size a little or there are no lulls you will need to learn how to duck dive to make it past the breaking waves. A duck dive is a method to get you and your board under the advancing wall of water. This is the most underestimated part of a surfer's skills.

Paddle towards the breaking wave and as it approaches sink the front of your board by raising your body as if you are doing a push-up. At the same time you need to push the nose of your board down under the wave. Bend your arms, keeping a firm hold of your board, take a breath and just as the wave is about to meet you, duck your head and whole body under it. Place your knee in the middle of the board and raise your other leg in the air.

A surfer successfully duck diving a wave that Tassy Swallow is riding. (Photo: Sarah Bunt)

Duck diving step 1.
(Photo: Approaching Lines)

Duck diving step 2.
(Photo: Approaching Lines)

When duck diving in bigger waves you can use your foot to push the board deeper under the water.
(Photo: Approaching Lines)

In theory your board should sink and you should pass under the advancing wave and appear on the other side. In practice you may find your board flying out behind you or between your legs so make sure you practise in small waves when there are no surfers behind or close to you. Mastering a duck dive takes a lot of practice. It pays dividends to watch how other surfers do it. Take a little time out on the beach on a bigger day and see how they time their 'duck' before the wave arrives so that the wave passes over them, leaving them to appear after the force of the water has passed. As with everything in surfing, it is all about practice, practise, practice.

Be Sure to Know the Rules

Now that you have progressed out into the line-up, there will be a lot more happening – waves breaking, surfers taking off close to you, so it is important to fully understand the rules of the line-up. This will help keep you and other surfers safe and mean you enjoy your surfing more. Be sure to follow the code laid out in Chapter 8. Also, don't be afraid to ask advice from other surfers. Everyone has been a beginner and you'll find most surfers are happy to offer a little guidance.

Having fun while riding a green wave. (Photo: Sarah Bunt)

Concentration is key. (Photo: Sarah Bunt)

CHAPTER 12

BASIC MANOEUVRES

The next step is to get to grips with the basics of how to control your board. This will help you stay in the right part of the wave as well as giving you the ability to stay out of the way of other surfers. In an increasingly busy line-up, it is essential to be able to avoid collisions and this basic form of board control is the root of all surfing manoeuvres.

A longboarder surfing 'down the line'. (Photo: Sarah Bunt)

Down The Line Surfing

When you're going along the open face, or trimming, experiment with subtly shifting your weight over either rail or board edge. You can do this by applying pressure through your toes and by very subtle changes in weight distribution from toes to heels. Remember to keep your knees bent, shoulders square and head pointing in the direction you want to go. It is a little like doing a subtle slalom on a skateboard or snowboard, only this is on a moving wave so it is much harder. The aim is to climb up the face of the wave to the top third and then drop down the face to the bottom third. This can help you to gain speed on smaller waves as each drop helps you gain momentum.

For example, a regular footer on a right is facing the wave and by applying subtle pressure through the toes, will climb the face. Then by gently releasing the pressure and leaning to the left, the board will drop down the face again. In doing so it will gain momentum and accelerate.

If you exaggerate your lean, you will either straighten out and head towards the beach or pull out, coming off the back of the wave – useful if you see that the wave is going to close out and end your ride or if there is an unavoidable obstruction such a rock or fellow surfer in your path.

The Bottom Turn

This is the most important manoeuvre in surfing as it sets up the ride and is the first turn that you will do on the wave, helping to generate drive and speed for the rest of the wave. A good bottom turn is a smooth and flowing arc, converting the momentum from the drop into speed for the next turn. The most stylish surfers all base their surfing around a good bottom turn.

A forehand bottom turn for a regular footer on a right: paddle into the wave, angling slightly to the right, pop and drop down the face. At this point you will be going right but angling towards the bottom of the wave. Your head will be looking down the line to where you want to go. By applying pressure through the toes to the inside rail and subtly leaning into the turn the board should enter an arc and begin to turn up the face, heading towards the top of the wave. Don't make

Josh Ward, down the line on his backhand. (Photo: Sarah Bunt)

Shaun Skilton bottom turning on his forehand. (Photo: Sarah Bunt)

again.

This rail-to-rail surfing is the basis of the modern style. It generates speed and flow and allows the surfer to convert the wave's momentum and steepness into acceleration and drive.

Backside or backhand surfing follows exactly the same principles – only this time the surfer will have his or her back to the wave. For example, a goofy footer surfing the same right would paddle into the wave, pop and begin to descend the face. Having their back to the wave, they would look over their right shoulder at where they are heading. The turn would begin with a subtle lean into the heel side or inside rail of the board with knees kept bent, a low centre of gravity and shoulders square. This induces the board to enter a steady arc, carving through the trough of the wave and turning to face back up the face of the wave. At this point the surfer would now be looking at the top of the wave where they want to go. By releasing the pressure on the rail the board will plane towards the top of the wave. Before the board reaches the top of the wave the goofy footer initiates a top turn by applying pressure to the outside* or toe side rail, which will then begin to bite into the wave face. At this point the surfer is looking back down the face, turning his or her upper body as the board begins to arc and smoothly carve through 90 degrees. The top turn finishes as the surfer starts to drop back down the face of the wave, gaining speed.

*When talking of inside and outside rails, the inside rail is the edge of the board that is in contact with the wave face, providing bite and stability. This obviously changes depending on which direction a surfer is travelling, whether it is a right or left and whether they are regular or goofy.

the angle too sharp or aim straight back up at the lip – at this stage the idea is to get to the top third of the wave again.

Once out of the bottom turn and heading back towards the top of the wave, release the pressure and lean on the inside rail and apply subtle pressure to the heel side, turning your head to look back towards the bottom of the wave again. This will cause the board to enter another arc and begin to turn. You will then begin a top turn where the board carves through a 90 degree turn and begins to drop down the face again. The exit of the top turn is similar to taking off at the start of your wave in that you will be dropping down the face, aiming for the bottom, with your head facing down the line at where you want to go, ready to lean into a bottom turn

The Cutback

When surfing down the line it is important to stay in the steep part of the wave close to the curl. This is where the maximum amount of drive and speed can be generated. Venture too far out on to the face and the steepness of the wave decreases, causing a drop in the amount of drive generated and the surfer to become bogged down. This is where the cutback comes in. The cutback is one of the fundamental building blocks of good surfing style, a turn that brings a surfer back into the pocket, next to the curl.

The essence of this manoeuvre is a sideways figure of eight. The surfer drops down the face to generate speed, then rises, sets the board on its rail and carves a turn that results in him or her coming back in the opposite direction, heading back towards the breaking part of the wave. The second part of the cutback happens immediately and is to get back out on to the face again. The surfer aims back up the face and again carves a turn by putting the board on its rail, compressing into the turn, turning his or her head to look where they want to go and putting the board through a full arc to come out facing back on to the open face again. A cutback should generate speed and drive and propel the surfer into the next manoeuvre.

The start of a cutback. (Photo: Sarah Bunt)

Nicola Bunt cutting back on her longboard. (Photo: Sarah Bunt)

CHAPTER 13

PROGRESSIVE MANOEUVRES

While the basic manoeuvres are the building blocks of surfing a wave, the progressive manoeuvres are a way that a surfer can show off his or her individual style and are something that become important when a surfer wants to take wave riding to a competitive level. These are the things that will differentiate between an intermediate and advanced surfer, and will rack up the points in contests.

Forehand Snaps

A snap is a quick tight turn performed at the top of the wave that allows the surfer to throw out an impressive fan of spray while also letting them reset their rail for their next turn. The higher up the face of the wave that you perform the snap, the more exciting the manoeuvre will look. The key to this turn is pushing your back foot out at just the right moment, thus causing the water to spray out from your fins. You want to perform a snap on a peeling wave at a steep section. It is essential that, as with any manoeuvre, you start with plenty of speed. Complete your bottom turn and point your board at a 45 degree angle towards the top of the wave. As you get to the top of the wave, let your upper body lead by opening out your shoulders and pointing your front arm back down the wave, then push your back leg out hard creating the snap part of the turn. Reposition the centre of your body back over your board and look down the line.

Roundhouse Cutbacks

This is a more accomplished version of the basic cutback that turns the simple manoeuvre into an impressive display of polished surfing. It fulfils the same basic function as a cutback but with an extra element of flair. This manoeuvre can be performed on both your forehand and backhand.

On your forehand, as with the snap, complete your bottom turn and head

A forehand snap by goofy footer Jeremy Bunt. (Photo: Sarah Bunt)

Josh Ward throws a fan of spray while performing a backhand snap. (Photo: Sarah Bunt)

back towards the top of the wave. However, this time rather than snapping the board, push down with your back foot in a longer smoother motion while pointing your front arm back towards the curl of the wave. It is very important that you are also looking back in this direction, too, and as the foam ball part of the wave comes into view you need to maintain focus on this, as this is where you want to hit the wave with your board. As your board connects with the lip of the curl, bring your front shoulder and arm down in front of your body sharply, which will bring the rest of your body back down into the fastest part of the wave.

The backside roundhouse is considered an easier manoeuvre to perform as for the most part you are facing the wave and therefore able to see where you need to be. Complete your bottom turn and when you are nearing the top of the wave, lean on the toe side of the rail and bend your knees, look towards the curl of the wave and place your trailing hand in the water to act as a pivot. The foam ball will now be in front of you. Aim your board towards the lip of the curl; once you've hit it, point your front arm towards the bottom of the wave and push out with your back foot. You should have plenty of momentum generated from hitting the lip to enable you to bring your board down fairly easily. Point your board back down the line of the wave and set up for your next manoeuvre.

Floaters

The floater serves two purposes: it is a great way of getting past a breaking section and back on to the clean face of the wave, and it can also look really impressive when performed on a large powerful wave. It is not something that you can perform on any wave as you need an appropriate section to hit and 'float' over. If you are going down the line of a wave and see a part of the wave ahead of you that has broken, this is an opportunity to do a floater.

On your forehand, as you approach the section, you need to do your bottom turn in the middle of the wave and then aim back up at a 30 degree angle to the point where the whitewater of the oncoming section meets the green of the wave. Using the curl as a ramp, you then need to 'place' your board on the roof of the wave and glide over the section while keeping your body weight low. At this point you will have your weight over your toe edge but you will need to transfer it to your heel edge to maintain your momentum and to keep you on the top of the wave. As you near the end of the section, move your weight forward and guide your board smoothly back on to the green face of the wave. If the wave is steep, you may need to shift your weight back a little at this point to avoid nosediving your board.

On your backhand, the key is being able to generate enough speed, so stay high on the fastest part of the wave, bottom turning at the last minute in the middle of the wave. Hit the lip of the approaching section and again, using the lip as a ramp, place your board on the top of the wave. It is really important at this point to move your weight back to your heel edge and forward to avoid simply coming off the back of the wave. As with a forehand floater, when you get to the end of the section, adjust your weight forward and ride out using the lip.

Barrels

The barrel is considered the holy grail of surfing as it is one of the hardest things to perfect. This combined with the fact that it requires a steep, perfect tubing wave makes it one of the most elusive manoeuvres in surfing but also one of the most rewarding if executed well. Good barrel riding requires a combination of positioning and speed management and takes a long time to master.

Once you have dropped into a wave

Setting up for a forehand roundhouse cutback. (Photo: Sarah Bunt)

A young ripper floating over a section. (Photo: Sarah Bunt)

Chops Lascelles tucking into a forehand barrel. (Photo: Sarah Bunt)

on your forehand and you see a steep section ahead of you that looks like it is going to barrel, you need to pump your board down the line and put yourself in the perfect position so that the lip of the wave throws over your head. You then have to make the split second decision of how quickly the barrel is moving and work out whether you have to stall to remain in the tube by planting your hand in the wall of the wave and moving your weight back or race to ensure a clean exit from the barrel by continuing to pump your board.

In order to get barrelled on your backhand, the most commonly used technique is the 'pig dog'. This involves dropping into a backhand wave and keeping your trailing hand on the rail of your board while dragging your front hand through the wall of the wave and allowing the lip to throw over you. The pig dog positioning helps you maintain board stability while also letting you stall to remain in the barrel. Again, if you need to race through a rapidly peeling barrel, you can start pumping your board to enable you to surf out cleanly.

Frontside Airs

Airs or aerials are a fairly recent addition to the repertoire of surfing manoeuvres but have become more and more popular in recent times as 'flying above the lip' is what most young surfers aspire to achieve. They are also a manoeuvre that is suited to small onshore conditions so it is a great thing to practise when conditions are less than perfect. The fundamentals are not dissimilar to those of a floater in that you need a section to

hit, however this time your aim is to launch your surfboard and yourself into the air.

Approach the oncoming section as you would with a floater and, going as fast as you can, aim the board at the lip you are going to hit and carry the momentum into the air rather than on to the roof of the wave. You do this by pushing off the tail of your board and making sure it is flat on the lip when you take off.

Once airborne you need to turn the

Robin Kent pig-dogging through a backhand barrel. (Photo: Sarah Bunt)

nose of your board so that it is facing the beach and pull your knees into your chest while remaining centred over the top of your board. Extend your legs, pick your landing spot and bend your knees to absorb the impact.

Barrels aren't just for shortboarders, Ben Skinner in the tube on his longboard. (Photo: Sarah Bunt)

Jonny Marshall going deep. (Photo: Sarah Bunt)

Brandon Hawkins tail high in the air. (Photo: Xcel)

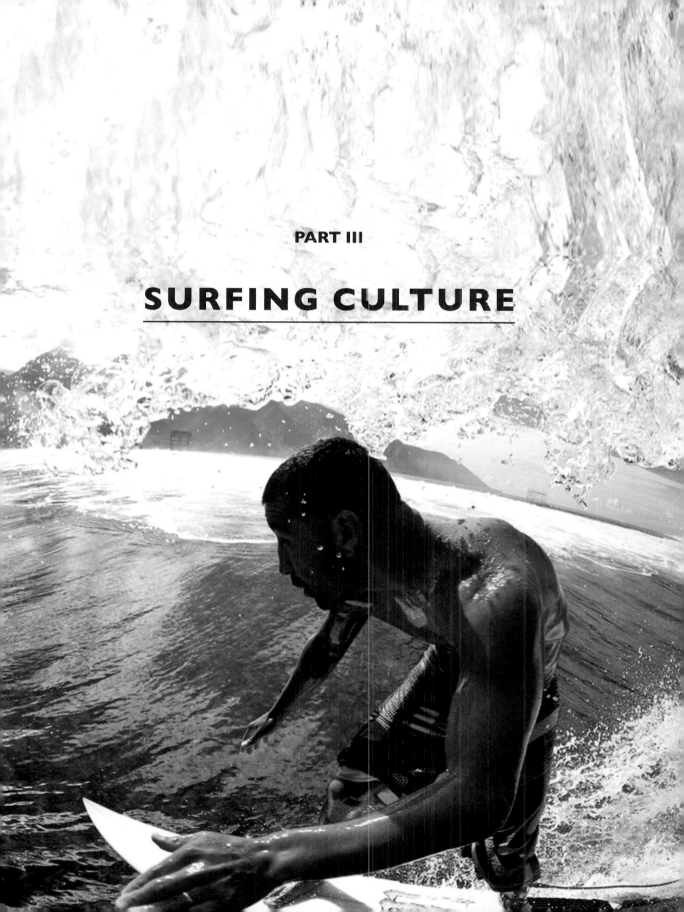

PART III

SURFING CULTURE

CHAPTER 14

SURF FIT

There's an old saying that goes 'the best way to get surf fit is to surf'. This is because the muscles involved in surfing are ones seldom used in daily life and general sport and fitness regimes. Even the fittest person will find him or herself exhausted after a short time in the surf, unless they have trained specifically for paddling and popping. Not everyone has access to the beach every day to build up those muscle groups needed to help surf stamina, however most people do have access to a swimming pool, and there are swim drills that can help build stamina and strength to make surfing easier.

Salim Ahmed is the founder of swimming training company SwimLab and is a keen surfer and open water swimmer. SwimLab runs SwimClinic weekends at the Watergate Bay Hotel in Cornwall, and coaching sessions in Hampton and Shepperton Lake, both in Middlesex, and the Italian Riviera.

'Having swum for over forty-five years, and surfed for thirty-five of them, I've discovered a weird but essential relationship,' says Salim. 'We take the swimming bit for granted. After all, you have your board to save your life, don't you? Get caught in a rip, and you can ride it out and paddle out of it (in theory). The only time we think about swimming is when our leash breaks out back or in the impact zone. Getting your swim stroke fine-tuned could save your life in that situation. What we sometimes forget as surfers is that a strong swim regime combined with technique can not only save your life, but enhance your surfing immeasurably.'

To Get Swim Fit

Paddling on a board is very different to swimming without one but many of the basic drills can add strength to your paddle out, and make the difference when paddling for that elusive wave. With strong swim fitness, you could be catching waves others can't:

1. Always start a session with one or two lengths of front crawl leg kick only using a float. We never use those legs, and they can make all the difference once you're off the board.

2. Swim 10 × 25 front crawl as a warm-up. Concentrate on a long drawn out stroke, reaching right out with each arm stroke.

3. Swim 30 × 25 front crawl, alternating from a comfortable cruise to a demo-sprint (at 65 to 70 per cent effort). Use the slow length to recover, before picking up the speed largely through a slight increase in kick rate.

4. Swim twelve lengths alternating a head up, water polo-style, front crawl paddle looking straight ahead, with three normal lengths of front crawl with head down and breathing to the side.

5. Finally, end with six lengths of breaststroke, extending the glide. Aim to work at completing each length with fifteen strokes or less.

To Get out of Trouble

1. Build lung capacity by a bit of unstructured play. Swim underwater for as far as you can. Note and build on it. Perfect practice for being held down! I know!

2. Keep your cool if your leash snaps; you are buoyant with a wetsuit. Keep a steady rhythm to your stroke, and don't over kick. Ninety per cent of your forward momentum comes from your upper body! Spot direction every ten to fifteen strokes.

3. Don't fight the rip or the waves. Ride with them.

Style Drill

1. Bilateral breathing – learn how to breathe every three strokes to alternating sides. You can then breathe every two strokes to whichever side you like depending on the waves.

2. Perfect a high elbow efficient stroke.

The pool drill is to take a float, start with a push off and with just legs kicking. After three seconds, engage your arms. After your first arm stroke, recover back over while trailing your fingernails over the surface of the flat pool water. This will automatically pull your arm into an Olympian swimmer-style stroke. Obviously the objective is to swim with a high elbow stroke as high as the chop conditions will allow.

3. Glide and reach with every stroke.

Surf Balance

Balance is also an important element in surfing and there are a number of ways a surfer can improve his or her twitch response out of the water.

Balance Ball

These soft balls have become a really popular multipurpose exercise tool for surfers from learners to professionals. They can be used to help with a variety of different skills that are required to improve an individual's surfing ability. A beginner surfer can use the balance ball to help with improving their pop-ups by performing a push-up with their hands on the balance ball rather than on the floor as this emulates the unstable nature of trying to pop up on a wave. Pro surfers will use a balance ball as part of their pre-heat warm-up in order to fine-tune their core stability and help prepare them mentally for competition.

Indo Board

A popular downtime activity for surfers, the Indo Board is a great way to practise balance for all types of surfing on dry land. As with the balance ball, it is a great way to increase core strength in a fun way. Longboard techniques such as cross stepping and nose-riding can be practised as well as shortboard style flips and ollies.

Yoga

Yoga is considered one of the best things to complement surfing as, among countless other benefits, it helps to increase that all-important flexibility and can counterbalance some of the demands that surfing can put on your body, helping to correct the stiffening of certain areas and freeing you up to surf with more fluidity. Most top professional surfers will practise yoga as part of their training and pre-contest preparation.

Helen Clare is an experienced and passionate yoga teacher who teaches classes in Cornwall and leads yoga retreats around the world, often combined with surfing. A keen surfer, she is dedicated to spreading the health benefits of yoga and works closely with many athletes as part of their cross-training, injury prevention and therapy. Helen teaches a Vnyasa flow style of yoga – a dynamic, flowing style in which each movement is timed with the breath – perfect for surfers to become more aware of the power of their breathing. It can be as challenging as required and each class combines a combination of strengthening and flexibity enhancing poses, sequenced in a purposeful flow, creating a feeling of rhythm and progression. Here she explains the benefits of a yoga practice to complement surfing:

'I see a great connection between surfing and yoga – they are both like moving meditation; both require a connection between the mind, body and breathing; and both demand physical strength and flexibility. They are both solo practices, allowing you to focus completely on your own body, mind and emotions.'

Surfing and yoga work together incredibly well – a regular yoga practice will increase your lung capacity, improve your flexibility and help increase strength, release tension and develop mental focus. Yoga will add strength to the back muscles, aiding ease in paddling, ansd also strengthen the core muscles to protect the lower back and the hips – a surfer's centre of power. Yoga can help you safely maintain upper body strength when you're out of the water and develop leg strength in balancing poses. Above all, it will allow you to release built up tension in the hips, hamstrings, neck, back and shoulders that if left can cause pain and injury.

This series of simple daily postures can help keep your body and mind surf-ready.

WHAT: Downward facing dog
WHY: Great for re-lengthening the spine and back muscles, releasing tension in hamstrings and calves. This pose is great to do at any time of day, and is always the first pose I do in the morning.
HOW: Start on your hands and knees, push into your hands to lift the knees and guide your hips up and back, lengthening your spine. Only then start to think about lowering your heels towards the ground. If your hamstrings are tight, which in surfers is very likely, then this pose will be hard at first – primarily think about lengthening the back and arms by keeping a bend in the knees. Hold for around five breaths.

WHAT: Low lunge
WHY: Great for releasing tension in the

Downward facing dog. (Photo: Dougie Reid/Helen Clare Yoga)

Pyramid step 1. (Photo: Dougie Reid/Helen Clare Yoga)

Low lunge. (Photo: Dougie Reid/Helen Clare Yoga)

Pyramid step 2. (Photo: Dougie Reid/Helen Clare Yoga)

hip flexors, a common area of tension in surfers

HOW: From down dog, step one foot forward, bringing the ankle under the knee. Place your hands on your front thigh and lower your tail bone toward the ground as you sink your hips until you feel a deep but comfortable stretch in the front of your hip. Your hands can also be on the floor or resting on blocks either side of you. Your front knee should be above your ankle, or you can take it slightly past the ankle to increase the

Pyramid step 3. (Photo: Dougie Reid/Helen Clare Yoga)

stretch in the calf and Achilles. Use a blanket under your back knee for added comfort. Take five deep slow breaths, focusing on the hip flexors in the front of the hip of the back leg, exhaling out the tension.

WHAT: Side stretch lunge
WHY: This pose offers a great side body stretch that can go all the way down from your latissimus dorsi – under your armpits – into the hip, stretching into the tensor fasciae latae muscle, which attaches to the IT band and the quadratus lumborum (QLs) in the lower back (this pair of muscles either side of your lower spine will undoubtedly be tight from paddling).
HOW: From the low lunge take your hands to your hips and align hip over knee and knee over ankle. Reach up, hold your right wrist and stretch over to the left. Take two or three breaths here.

WHAT: Runner's stretch
WHY: This pose starts to deepen the stretch into the centre of the hamstrings, helping to re-lengthen the muscles. The hamstrings contract when you paddle, so it is a good idea to stretch them out post-surf to prevent you feeling stiff later on.
HOW: From the side stretch lunge, come up and take your hands to the ground and press your front toes down, lengthening the front leg – this will provide a nice stretch through the front of the ankle and shin. Then, bend the left knee and lift the toes, draw back the hip before beginning to straighten the leg to your own degree, protecting the back of the knee. Keep flexing the toes back and drawing the hip into the socket.

WHAT: Pyramid
WHY: Releasing tight hamstrings
HOW: From a low lunge position, step

Cobra step 1. (Photo: Dougie Reid/Helen Clare Yoga)

Cobra step 2. (Photo: Dougie Reid/Helen Clare Yoga)

Up dog. (Photo: Dougie Reid/Helen Clare Yoga)

Eagle arms. (Photo: Dougie Reid/Helen Clare Yoga)

the back foot forward, place your hands on your hips and come up halfway. Extend your spine by looking forwards and level your hips. Remain here, or take your hands to the floor or rest them on blocks, keep the spine long for another breath before exhaling and folding over your front leg to your own degree. Find the stretch in the belly of the hamstrings, keeping a bend in the front knee as required. For an additional shoulder stretch, interlace your fingers behind your back. Hold for five breaths, replace your hands back on your hips and inhale up with a long spine, navel drawing in.

WHAT: Revolved triangle
WHY: This continues to lengthen the hamstrings and ease out tension in the gluteus medius, minimus and piriformis – external hip rotating muscles that help us to turn. The twisting action of this pose is fantastic for increasing your range of motion, which will add drive into your cutbacks.
HOW: From pyramid pose, widen the stance slightly by moving the back foot back an inch or two, keeping the heel down. If your right foot is in front, keep your right hand on your hip and take the left hand to the floor or on to a block.

Revolve slowly to the right, keeping the hips level, then if comfortable extend your arm up.

WHAT: Cobra/up dog
WHY: This opens the chest and draws back the shoulders – developing a perfect paddling position.
HOW: On your front, place your hands either side of your chest. Roll back your shoulders to lift your chest but keep your elbows bent and hugging in. Relax your shoulders down away from your ears. Press the tops of your feet into the ground. If your back is feeling more flexible take the opportunity to come up higher – just keep your shoulders away from your ears, visualizing the shoulder blades moving down. Take five breaths.

WHAT: Eagle arms
WHY: This arm position provides a stretch for the rhomboids, trapezius and latissimus dorsi in the back and shoulders.
HOW: Sit with legs crossed, or for those with more flexible hips cross and stack the knees. Either way, make sure your sitting bones are both comfortably grounded. Sit on a blanket or cushion if sitting is uncomfortable. Cross your arms

and begin to wrap your forearms and wrists to your own degree – this will be affected by tightness in the back and shoulders. Push the elbows away from you to go deeper. Take five to ten breaths. Switch the cross of your legs and arms.

WHAT: Pigeon
WHY: Great for: hips! This is an intense stretch for the gluteals and the deeper piriformis. All the hip muscles get tight from paddling, which if left can lead to back pain and knee problems. This pose gets deep and releases tension in the piriformis muscle, one of the main external hip rotators.
HOW: Move into this pose extra slowly, especially if you have any knee issues, due to the hip flexion and body weight over the knee. Begin in down dog or on hands and knees, then bring your right foot towards your left hand. Bring your shin to the ground with your right foot by your left hip. Check your back leg is out straight behind you and your hips are level, no matter how high they are! With tight hips you won't get them both to the ground – support yourself with a blanket roll or cushion under the right hip. Start upright then extend your torso forward. Take five to fifteen breaths, enjoy a deep

Pigeon step 1. (Photo: Dougie Reid/Helen Clare Yoga)

Pigeon step 2. (Photo: Dougie Reid/Helen Clare Yoga)

Bridge. (Photo: Dougie Reid/Helen Clare Yoga)

and developing focus, yoga allows your body to relax and replenish. Conscious relaxation is easier when muscles have been stretched out, so take the time to do this pose for five minutes at the end. HOW: Mentally scan through your whole body and encourage each area to relax. Give yourself this time to rejuvenate and you will recover in between surfs.

Lower back pain is common in surfers because of the contraction of the back muscles when paddling, in addition to the contraction of the hips and hamstrings. The best way to relieve and reduce low back pain is to release tension in the hips through mindful stretching.

Lay on your back with your feet flat on a wall in front of you. Cross one ankle over the other thigh and flex your toes back towards your knee in a figure four shape. To increase the stretch move closer in towards the wall, to reduce it move out further. This is a great easy stretch for the external hip rotators and gluteus muscles that doesn't take a lot of energy – perfect for last thing at night before the next day's surf.

stretch but come up if too intense. Repeat on the other side.

WHAT: Bridge
WHY: Great for opening the chest, drawing back the shoulders; stretching the psoas. Reverses the paddling position of the back and shoulders.
HOW: Lie on your back, bend your knees so that your ankles are under your knees and keep your feet parallel. Press your hands and feet down as you lift your hips up, keeping your head and neck on the ground. There are various arm positions for this pose, a nice addition is interlacing the fingers to gain extra lift. Keep the chest lifting the shoulder blades moving in toward each other. Take five breaths, one to three repetitions. Come down slowly and hug your knees in towards your chest.

WHAT: Relax
WHY: Aside from releasing tension through mindful stretching and strengthening, increasing lung capacity

CHAPTER 15

SURF TRAVEL

Travel has always been at the heart of surf culture. Ever since the first raft of modern wave-hunters pushed north from the southern California heartlands to the empty point waves of Malibu, the spirit of adventure and exploration has been ingrained within every surfer. The search for the perfect wave is a central mantra at the core of surf culture.

During the 1950s and early 1960s a winter trip to the hallowed grounds of Oahu became a badge of honour for California's wave riders. Surfers such as Greg Noll and a small clique, including the likes of Pat Curren, pushed out from the traditional base at Makaha on to the unexplored stretch of the North Shore.

In 1957 Noll and his crew were renting small shacks and running beat up cars up and down the Kamehameha Highway — then just a track — scoping the vast array of intimidating surf spots on offer. At a time when international travel was the preserve of the moneyed elite and big game hunters, surfers were boarding boats and jetliners bound for exotic locations, chasing a different kind of quarry.

In 1964 filmmaker Bruce Brown finished his latest project *The Endless Summer*. The movie snowballed in popularity, becoming an unexpected commercial hit and pulling audiences to such an extent that in 1966 it gained a

national release in the USA, becoming the first surf movie to get mainstream media coverage. Brown's opus followed Californian surfers Robert August and Mike Hynson as they traversed the world in search of the perfect wave.

On the southern tip of Africa they stumbled across a wave called Cape St Francis, a long peeling right-hand point break that would change surfing forever. The machine-like long hollow walls became emblematic of the perfect wave, and gave hope to surfers that the world was littered with surf spots still waiting to be discovered. All it would take was the spirit of adventure and exploration, a willingness to get out on the road and join the search.

Those inspired by the ethos of the search included two young Americans — Kevin Naughton and Craig Peterson. During the 1970s they embarked on expeditions to exotic destinations such as Liberia, Morocco, Senegal, France, Spain, Ireland, Mexico, Barbados and Fiji — mailing packages of handwritten text and slides back to Surfer Magazine extolling the joys and pains of life on the road. They pioneered many new breaks and spurred a generation to follow their lead.

By now there were surfers trekking through every corner of the globe, from civil war-torn Central America, to the freezing cedar forests of Vancouver Island in Canada. Tapping into this ethos the surf brand Rip Curl started an iconic advertising campaign called The Search.

Surf travel isn't just about warm water. Surfers finding frozen perfection. (Photo: Xcel)

These print ads ran through the 1990s and seemed to encapsulate surf travel in a single colour photograph. These idealized images of flawless empty surf breaks teased, tempted and lured a generation to seek out new waves in tropical locales. Picture perfect barrels spinning down a reef somewhere near the equator, a lone surfer paddling towards the flawless line-up, added fuel to the fire that was driving the exploration of remote regions such as the Mentawai Island chain in Indonesia.

Today there are few regions left that surfers have not explored. This even extends into the coldest parts of the globe. However, the joy of surf travel remains and there is something joyous about paddling out at a new break with a fresh backdrop to drink in.

South-west France: warm water and fun waves. (Photo: Kate Czuczman)

For Beginners

Travel isn't just for the experienced surfer. Sometimes a good surf trip is just what is needed to help kickstart your surfing. Look for a beach break with a surf school or surf coach with an excellent reputation.

Cornwall, UK

The long beaches of Perranporth Godrevy, Fistral and Watergate are perfect for learning on. Surf schools operate off these beaches and they are lifeguard-protected by the RNLI during the peak summer season.

France

Looking a little further afield, the town of Biarritz has a number of beaches with varying exposure to swell, so there should always be somewhere with breaking waves. Anglet is an exposed stretch of sand divided by boulder groynes. It runs from VVF (*Village Vacances Famille*) to the south up to les Cavaliers – a potentially world class break that can offer great lefts and rights for more experienced surfers.

Morocco

The Atlantic coast of north-west Africa offers the perfect blend of adventure and exploration. There are a number of excellent surf camps that can act as a base and will drive surfers to suitable breaks to fit their surfing ability and offer any tuition required. While the air temperature is warm, the water still carries enough of a chill to warrant a 3/2 wetsuit. Head for the area around Taghazout or Tamraght close to Agadir for beginner friendly waves.

Costa Rica

The huge expanse of the Pacific is rarely still and the sandy beaches of Costa Rica

Cornwall is a great option for surfers of all ages and abilities. (Photo: Sarch Bunt)

Samantha Raine enjoying the mellow waves of Costa Rica with Surf Sistas, who specialize in surf courses and 'surfaris' at the best destinations across the planet. (Photo: Kate Czuczman)

All you need for surfing in warm water, a board and boardshorts. (Photo: Approaching Lines)

offer an excellent place for those taking the plunge to score consistent warm water waves. There are many excellent spots to head for including Playa Grande to the north of Tamarindo, which lies in a national park, plus Mal Pais, which has a huge stretch of beach and a number of surf schools operating. Both beaches are on the Nicoya Peninsula in the north-west of the country.

For the Intermediate Surfer

For those who have mastered the basics of riding the open face and turning, and feel they would like to push their skills on more challenging beaches, points and reef breaks, there are many great destinations.

Scotland

The north coast of Scotland is a great destination, with many surf breaks and a plethora of set-ups to explore. The water temperature ranges from about 5 or 6 degrees in the winter, through to about 14 in the summer. A good time to visit is the autumn when the water temperatures are not too low and the swells and winds are most consistent.

Good spots to try are the beaches at Melvich and Farr Bay. The break at Thurso East is challenging and best left to those with some reef experience, but on the other side of the river in front of the sea wall lies an excellent reef break that is still challenging but less critical.

Portugal

Ericeira is a small fishing village that nestles on the Atlantic, a warren of cobblestone lanes lined by whitewashed cottages. The geology of this stretch of coastline means that there are a number of excellent breaks in and around the village, varying from fun beaches, through long points and up to challenging reefs. Just to the north sits Coxos, a shallow and hollow reef, and on the edge of town is Ribeira d'Ilhas, a right hand point break that bears a remarkable similarity to Bells Beach in Australia. On the southern edge of town is Foz do Lizandro, a sandy beach with some excellent waves.

Sri Lanka

A popular destination for Northern Hemisphere surfers, Sri Lanka has two surfing seasons. The western coastline, home to the well-known destination Hikkadua, is predominantly offshore during November to April, while the eastern side around Arugam Bay is best from May to October. The island offers small to moderate-sized waves and warm water, getting quite crowded around the popular breaks but allowing plenty of room to head out in search of quieter spots.

Maldives

For those ready for some perfect reef and point waves, but within a 4 to 6ft size range, then the island chain of the Maldives is perfect. The Indian Ocean swells that arrive here are seldom huge, and average the head high range. Boats operate between breaks, shipping clients to the best breaks each day. Alternatively, stay at one of the resorts that have exclusive access to the waves they look out over.

For Experts

For those who really want to push their limits and experience some of the best waves on the planet these world famous breaks can offer incredible waves. However, this comes at a price and their notoriety will always attract crowds of surfers wanting to enjoy what they have to offer.

The North Shore, Oahu

This is the spiritual home of surfing. The coastline runs from Kahuku Point to Ka'ena Point and contains some of the most famous breaks in the surfing word, including Sunset Beach, Pipeline, Rocky Point, Off The Wall, Waimea and Haleiwa. All these spots are for experts only. They are heavy waves with rips and super-competitive crowds. However, there are a few spots where you can escape the crowd and score some great waves. Staying in a surfer-run homestead will help give you the inside track.

Bali, Indonesia

Home to some of our most iconic waves, names that spawned a generation of searchers: Uluwatu, Padang Padang, Impossibles, Bingin and Dreamland on the western side of the Bukit Peninsula through to Sanur Reef and Keramas on the east. Bali is still the region's biggest surf destination and the breaks are much more crowded these days, but with ultra-consistent swells coming out of the southern Indian Ocean, offshore winds and warm waters, it is hard to resist the allure of this magical island.

Hawai'i is a special place for expert surfers. (Photo: Ocean and Earth)

Fins-free in tropical Indonesia. (Photo: Ocean and Earth)

Cloudbreak, Fiji

The pro surfer's favourite, a reef that can offer ruler perfect hollow lefts from 3ft to 15ft. Discovered by Californian surfer Dave Clark and just across the water from the island of Tavarua, this remained a private break for decades, the exclusive domain of those staying at the luxury Tavarua Resort. Recent legal changes mean it is now open to all. Fill your boots, but watch out for the super-shallow inside section known as Shish Kebabs.

Jeffrey's Bay, South Africa

Considered by many of the best surfers in the world to be the ultimate right-hand point break, this is a spot that offers everything from huge carving walls through to speedy hollow racetracks. This wave can break for well over 400m from Boneyards on the outside, all the way through Supertubes and Impossibles to The Point. A ride here can last a leg burning three minutes and the locals have the spot wired, sharing the line-up with pods of dolphins performing on the waves while Great Whites are an ever-skulking danger.

Wave Pool/Artificial Waves

These are man-made arenas where all the forces creating the waves are artificial. They come in various different forms all with the aim of emulating the feeling of riding a wave in the ocean. The benefit of surfing in these purpose-built facilities is that a surfer can practise the same manoeuvre over and over again until it is perfected, a luxury never enjoyed by surfers before due to the ever-changing nature of the ocean and its swells.

Stationary Waves

Although there are many variations of artificial stationary waves including The Loop at the Retallick resort in Cornwall and The Wavehouse at Belmont Park in San Diego, these all work in a similar way. A shallow sheet of water is pushed uphill over a composite membrane designed to absorb any impact. These are ridden on short finless boards and the sensation is equally akin to that of snowboarding and skateboarding. The rider will aim to maintain their position on the ride, making subtle adjustments to their weight distribution to perform tricks and manoeuvres.

Wave Pools

Here a surfer will be able to ride a wave very similar to the ones that nature provides in the ocean and he or she can enjoy the same the experience. Everything from paddling, catching the wave, taking the drop and riding the face is the same, the difference is that these waves can be controlled by a person at the press of a button, rather than being at the mercy of Mother Nature.

In 2013 the team at Wavegarden unveiled its demonstration facility in the Basque Country in northern Spain. This design innovation creates two perfect waves (one left, one right) which break simultaneously as a mass of water is moved over a surface.

The same patented technology has been used at Surf Snowdonia lying deep in the Conwy Valley in North Wales. This amenity enables surfers of all levels to enjoy freesurf sessions as well as lessons from qualified instructors and more intense full day courses. A similar facility, The Wave, will open in Bristol in the near future.

CHAPTER 16

THE ENVIRONMENT

The word environment is used a lot but what exactly is it? The environment is made up of everything that surrounds us and everything that we interact with. Our immediate environment is the air we breathe, our places of work, the water we drink, our local beach … in fact everywhere you go or might go, all the elements within them. As humans we are also part of the environment and everything we do will have an effect on it.

Earth is in effect a huge sealed system, inhabited by many forms of life, like a huge fish tank. Whatever we do within it will have an effect, to a greater or lesser extent, on the organisms and ecosystems around us. The coastal environment is particularly diverse and contains a huge array of plants, fish, birds and other organisms.

As surfers we spend a lot of time in and around the ocean fringes and it is inspiring to see the diverse nature all across the UK.

Two of the most frequent visitors to the line-up are the common seal and the grey seal. These can appear all around the coastline but the best places to see them are Scotland, the east coast, Wales, Devon and Cornwall. They are pretty inquisitive mammals and will often approach surfers in the water to check them out. They can also be seen hauling out on rocks and isolated beaches.

Don't be surprised to see a fin appearing when you're out in British waters. Most of the time it will be a

Clean seas are important to surfers of all ages. (Photo: Sarah Bunt)

bottlenose dolphin (*Tursiops truncatus*), welcome visitors along the shores of Cornwall where they can be seen in large pods, occasionally coming into shallow waters and surfing waves. Risso's dolphin (*Grampus griseus*) and common dolphins (*Delphinus delphis*) are also occasionally sighted.

Other larger interlopers include porpoises, whales and basking sharks. Porpoises are smaller relatives of dolphins and spend most of their time hunting further out at sea, so you might need your binoculars to spot them. Although basking sharks (Cetorhinus maximus) are the second biggest species of shark in the world, they are true gentle giants. They feed in the same way as many species of whale – by filtering plankton

out of the water. These incredible creatures were hunted nearly to the point of extinction so are now quite rare in our waters, but can be spotted off the coast of west Cornwall (try Sennen Cove or Porthcurno) and Scotland through the summer. Various species of whales can also be seen in the coastal waters around the UK. A great place to spot them is off the north coast of Scotland, where they navigate between the mainland and Orkney, which was named after the orca or killer whales. Species include minke whales, sperm whales, pilot whales or even killer whales. Even if you don't live in any of the areas listed, keep your eyes open as these marine mammals can crop up anywhere along Britain's coastline.

Waste Products

Most of the products a household buys in its weekly shop goes into the waste bin when it is finished. Some substances, such as bleaches and disinfectants, are designed to be poured down the sink or toilet. These products all go into the environment and fall into two categories: biodegradable materials such as paper packaging, waste food, and certain chemicals will eventually break down in the environment; non-biodegradable waste such as plastics, metals and certain chemicals will stay in the environment. Both degradable and non-biodegradable substances can cause pollution and affect plants and animals. Dolphins can get caught up in discarded fishing nets, seals can get snared by the looped plastic packaging that holds cans together and beachcombers may even tread on a rusty can washed on to the shore.

Plastic marine pollution is a hot topic with environmentalists and scientists as millions of tonnes of plastic waste currently circulate within the oceanic currents. It is worth taking a moment to think about the fact that we are still digging Roman coins, glassware and even leather sandals out of the ground. Imagine how long it may take plastic waste such as bottles to break down.

Pollution and Sewage

Unfortunately, for years the ocean has been seen as a convenient place to dispose of waste. Some authorities assumed that the oceans were so huge that pollution would just disappear. We now know that this is not true. Everything we put into the environment has an effect, no matter how small.

Sewage is made up of everything that goes down the toilet as well as waste

Waste caught in a grill at the end of a sewage overflow pipe. (Photo: SAS)

from sinks. At bathing beaches sewage outfalls should at least have had some basic processing before being dumped into the sea, but for years raw sewage was discharged around the coastline. This situation has now improved to the point where the quality at many bathing beaches is much better. However, surf breaks aren't just located on bathing beaches, many are found away from the tourist magnets and some are close to sewage outfalls. For example, Porthleven in Cornwall has a reefbreak close to its harbour, considered one of the best in the UK. However, as it is not designated as a swimming beach water quality is not tested or subject to pollution control.

Combined Sewer Overflows (CSOs)

There are approximately 31,000 combined sewer overflows (CSOs) around the UK. Their sole purpose is to discharge untreated human sewage and waste water when the sewerage system is overloaded, as in after a period of heavy rain. CSOs act as emergency discharge valves in our sewerage system, discharging untreated sewage and waste water when the system comes close to bursting, supposedly during periods of intense rainfall. Without CSOs, sewage could start backing up in our houses and gardens, so they are a vital part of our sewerage infrastructure. Environmental Campaign group Surfers Against Sewage (SAS) has become increasingly concerned that CSOs are being used to regularly dispose of untreated sewage, even during times of low rainfall or none at all. In theory, CSOs should only discharge a maximum of three times per bathing season (May–September) but worryingly many CSOs discharge far more frequently than this. This has become an increasing problem during

Surfers and water users protesting about sewage being pumped into the sea at Godrevy Beach in Cornwall. (Photo: SAS)

Surfing Organizations

Surfers Against Sewage is a hugely successful environmental group formed by a band of surfers from the Cornish village of St Agnes. Angered by the polluted state of local beaches, they decided to do something about it. They formed the fledgling group back in 1990 because they were 'sick of getting sick' at their local surfing beaches. Their original aims were to clean up the three nearby breaks, but within four years they had nearly 15,000 members and expanded into a national organization that now liaises with governments at national level as well as speaking at conferences across the globe. SAS has local events and activists across the UK.

The Surfrider Foundation was formed in America in the 1984 and is now the world's largest grass roots environmental group. The strength of the group is that it has a network of local 'chapters', which work at a local level. It sued polluters through the court system as well as initiating a system of water testing that the government itself refused to instigate.

the peak summer tourist period where sewage has been discharged on to beaches packed with bathers.

Other Forms of Pollution

Effects from pollution can be immediate and attract a lot of attention, like when an oil tanker sinks. But it can also be a gradual thing. If factories are discharging waste into the sea, species of fish may become sick and gradually disappear. Some pollution can be invisible. Sandside Bay in Scotland is one of the best surf breaks in Caithness. Unfortunately it is located near Dounreay nuclear power plant. Signs on the beach warn of radioactive particles present and the dangers of playing in the sand.

Environmental Organizations

Some people felt so strongly about the damage being done to the environment that they formed groups to try to do something about it.

A sign at Sandside Beach warning surfers and beach users of the presence of radioactive particles disposed into the sea by Dounreay power station. (Photo: Tim Nunn/The Plastic Project)

THE ENVIRONMENT

In 1990, top surfer Tom Curren opened a European chapter that is active in France and mainland Europe.

Marine Conservation Society

The MCS runs some excellent schemes including Adopt a Beach and Beach Watch. They also do beach clean ups and have a really useful Good Beach Guide (www.goodbeachguide.co.uk).

2 Minute Beach Clean

This is a simple organization with a simple ethos. Every time you visit the beach take two minutes to collect the litter you see and through these small actions big things will be achieved. Founded by surfer Martin Dorey, the idea has spread through social media, striking a chord with thousands of beach goers.

2 Minute Beach Clean.

Plastic washed up on an otherwise beautiful surfing beach. It takes just two minutes to make a difference. (Photo: 2 Minute Beach Clean)

A surfer about to enter the water at a litter-filled beach. (Photo: SAS)

The mission of The Plastic Project is to create a visual survey of marine litter in the wildest parts of the world. (Photo: Tim Nunn/The Plastic Project)

CHAPTER 17

SURF CONTESTS

Contest Structure

Surf competitions can vary in how they are run, however they all follow the same general structure of a knockout formula starting with heats and culminating with a final and an eventual winner. Although some heats in top-level contests will have as few as two surfers in them, they usually consist of four surfers who are scored on each wave they catch. They can catch as many waves as they want but only get scored on their best two waves.

The waves are scored on several elements including commitment and degree of difficulty, innovation and progressive manoeuvres, combination of major manoeuvres and how much speed, power and flow the surfer has displayed on the wave. Each wave is scored out of ten by a panel of judges and a surfer can score a maximum of twenty points per heat. The top two surfers from each heat (one surfer if it is a two-person heat) will progress to the next round.

World tour surfing events will usually use a priority system whereby each surfer takes it in turn to have the pick of whichever wave they want. If another surfer impedes on this they will be penalized.

Preparing for a Contest

It is important that a surfer is prepared both mentally and physically for competition. As with any sport, this involves good nutrition prior to the event plus a well-planned and focused fitness plan. A surfer will spend time prior to his or her heat assessing the surf conditions and the judging criteria. A lot of the top professionals will travel with a coach who will help them with their pre-heat preparation.

Surf Contest Strategy

Professional competitive surfers will all vary in their approach to surfing a heat. Some will keep busy and try to catch as many waves as they can while others will take a more patient approach and wait for the best waves. Some surfers have been known to try to psych out their competitors by paddling aggressively around the line-out or even by trying to talk to their competitors during a heat.

Progressive surfing in a contest. (Photo: Sarah Bunt)

Solid size swell at a local competition. (Photo: Sarah Bunt)

Fun Contests

There are an increasing number of surf gatherings that follow a competitive format, but which have the emphasis firmly on having a good time. Some wave riders are put off by the competitiveness of some events and these cater to an increasing number who wish to hang out and enjoy the good vibes.

The Slyder Cup is an annual event for those who enjoy riding all kinds of wave craft, the only criteria is that they have to be finless. This can include body surfing, surf mats, bellyboards, alaia and paipos. The emphasis is on good vibes all round, although there is a competition element with a winner crowned in each category as well as an overall Slyder Cup Champion.

Other Events

The Girls Ten Board Challenge is an event for women surfers who draw lots prior to each heat to see which surfboard they'll be riding from an array of assembled styles, sizes and fin combinations.

Swellboard Shootout is a team event where surfers wear fancy dress and ride foam learner boards.

Local Contests

There are many local surf contests around the UK open to all comers. You don't need to be a dedicated professional or aspiring competitive surfer – if you just fancy having a go you can enter online through the event website and pull on a contest jersey. They usually have categories for men and women as well as different age groupings. Most are for shortboarders, however some also have longboard categories. You will find a local event through your local surf shop – usually the hub for most local comps. Events such as these include The Cornish and Open, the UK's longest running surf contest, which takes place in Porthtowan, Cornwall, each summer. The event first ran in 1966 and was one of Europe's first contests. Another is the Saltburn Open that takes place each September in Saltburn-by-the-Sea in Cleveland and is one of the North-east's longest running events. For more details visit http://saltburnsurfshop.co.uk

BLU Longboard Tour

This is a series of local events exclusively for longboard riders run by the British Longboard Union. They take place in Saunton, North Devon; Freshwater West

Some contests encourage good vibes as well as good rides. (Photo: Sarah Bunt)

Body surfer Jo Reed practising for the Slyder Cup. (Photo: Sarah Bunt)

The Slyder Cup finalists with their alternative wave riding craft. (Photo: Approaching Lines/Mat Arney)

in Wales; and Crantock, Perranporth and Fistral in Cornwall. Each event has a number of categories with a winner in each. These include open, ladies, girls under-18, boys under-18, plus the under-16s cadet division. There is also a single fin division, a masters and grand masters. There is a cumulative points system leading to the crowning of a national champion in each division.

Grom Search

The Rip Curl Grom Search is a series of events aiming to identify the best under-16 male and female surfers. The search is comprised of three events taking place at Croyde Bay in North Devon, Freshwater West in Wales and Watergate Bay in Cornwall. A combination of a surfer's best two results will identify two male and female surfers who will then go on to represent the UK in the European finals somewhere in Europe, and battle to earn a place in the Rip Curl Grom Search World Finals. Previous Grom Search winners include top professionals Gabriel Medina, Matt Wilkinson, Owen Wright and six times world champion Stephanie Gilmore.

National Contests

The English, Scottish and Welsh Surfing Federations all hold annual national championships that are open to members of each respective federation. These events are normally held in late spring at one of each of the three regions top surfing spots.

Each event has a number of divisions including men's and women's shortboard, men's and women's longboard, plus various age categories. These contests can help to select the surfers who will represent their national teams at the EuroSurf and EuroJunior Surfing Championships.

British National Surfing Championships

Surfing GB is the designated national governing body for surfing in the UK and is mandated by the International Surfing Association (ISA) to oversee the sport. As such, it is responsible for operating the British Schools, British Interclubs and British National Surfing Championships. It also supports the BUCS Student Championships. Surfing GB's focus is

You're never too young to start competing. (Photo: Sarah Bunt)

Nicola Bunt on the nose in a longboard competition. (Photo: Sarah Bunt)

'amateur', without prize money. Its focus is for events at all levels to form part of a performance pathway that can ultimately lead to international success as well as a thriving domestic scene.

UK Professional Surf Tour

UKPST is a series of events held at different surf spots around the UK offering surfers a chance to compete for individual event wins, plus the overall Pro Surf Tour title. Each event offers a small amount of prize money. Check out the website for more details and an up-to-date list of events.

European Championships

Each national federation sends a squad of surfers to the bi-annual ESF Eurosurf Championships. The English, Welsh and Scottish Federations have the responsibility for selecting a team from the pool of surfers who qualify. The venue for each championships rotates between European federations.

ISA World Surfing Games

The International Surfing Association is the governing body responsible for amateur surfing and is recognised as such by the International Olympic Committee. It overseas the sport globally and runs the annual World Surfing Games. The British team competes at this event where gold, silver, bronze and copper medals are awarded to national teams and individual champions, with surfers competing for the honour of representing their countries and national colours, in the true nature of surfing's aloha spirit and fair play. Eligible surfers are selected under the guidance of Surfing GB.

Elite International Contests

Elite professional surfing is overseen by the World Surfing League (WSL), the governing body responsible for the Men's and Women's Championship Tour, Qualifying Tour, Big Wave Tour and Longboard Tour.

The men's WSL World Qualifying Series is a circuit of events offering each surfer a chance to not only win the contest and prize money, but also to accumulate enough points to qualify for the top tier of world competitive surfing, the illustrious World Championship Tour (WCT). Each event has a number of points on offer for each surfer, depending on where they finish. A WSL 1000 has 1,000 points on offer for the winner, a WSL 6000 offers 6,000 and a WSL 10,000 offers 10,000 to the winner. Second, third and fourth score commensurate points. WQS surfers' best five results are combined to produce their final point totals. The top ten surfers ranked on the year-end WSL WQS rankings will advance on to the WCT to join the twenty-two best ranked surfers on the WCT, along with two wildcard surfers, to make a total of thirty-four WCT competitors.

There are more than thirty events in the Qualifying Series. Some of the stops were previously on the WCT circuit and have a long and illustrious history. These include the Sunset Pro on Oahu in Hawaii, the Gunston 500 (now the Ballito Pro) in Durban, South Africa, the Burleigh Heads Pro, Queensland in Australia, the Lacanau Pro in France and the Huntington Beach Pro in California. There are also events in Japan, Brazil, Indonesia, Argentina, Martinique, Spain and the Philippines.

The women's WSL World Qualifying Series follows a similar format in that there are fourteen events, WQS surfers' best five results are combined to produce their year-end points total and the top six surfers ranked on the WSL Women's Rankings at the end of the year advance on to the women's Championship Tour.

WSL WCT

The men's World Championship Tour is open to only the best thirty-four surfers on the planet. Qualification is a long and difficult task but those on the WCT get to compete on what is christened the 'Dream Tour'. The theory is that the contest circuit visits some of the best breaks on the planet. Stops include Snapper Rocks, Bells Beach, Cloudbreak, Jeffreys Bay, Teahupo'o, Trestles and Hossegor, with the finale being held at the iconic Pipeline on the North Shore of Oahu, Hawaii.

The women's World Championship Tour consists of the seventeen best competitive surfers on the planet. There are ten events on the women's WCT taking place at many of the same stops, including Snapper Rocks, Bells Beach, Cloudbreak, Trestles and Hossegor, with the finale being held at the iconic Honolua Bay on Maui, Hawaii. All events from the men's and women's WCT are streamed live in HD via the World Surf League website for free to a global audience.

Surfing World Champions

US surfer Kelly Slater is an eleven times men's World Surfing Champion, becoming one of sports' most dominant athletes. For some Slater is one of the greatest athletes of all time. That is not to say that his dominance in surfing was complete and Slater had many close rivals over the course of his career. He won his first title in 1992 and his latest in 2011. However, during his career rivals included Mick Fanning and Andy Irons, both winners of three World Championships each, plus Joel Parkinson, Gabriel Medina, C.J. Hobgood, Sunny Garcia, Mark Occhilupo and Derek Ho with a world title each. Slater is both the youngest (20) and oldest World Champion (39).

Other legendary World Champions include Mark Richards (×4) 1979, '80, '81 and '82; Tom Curren (×3) in 1985, '86 and '90; and Tom Carroll (×2) 1983 and '84.

In women's surfing there have been some dominant champions who have pushed the envelope of just what is possible in the water and helped inspire a new generation of up and coming female wave riders.

Australian surfer Layne Beachley's currently the most successful champion with seven world titles between 1998 and 2006 – six of which were consecutive. Hot on her tail is fellow Aussie Stephanie Gilmore, who is currently on six world crowns, claiming the first in her rookie season of 2007. Steph is the most high profile female surfer with an appeal that has crossed over into mainstream media. She starred in a documentary about her rise to the upper echelons of wave riding called Stephanie in the Water that has won many awards at film festivals across the globe.

Other multiple World Champions include Lisa Andersen (×4) 1994, '95, '96 and '97; Wendy Botha (×4) 1987, '89, '91 and '92; Freida Zamba (×4) 1984, '85, '86 and '88; Margo Oberg (×3) 1977, '80 and '81 plus Carissa Moore (×3) 2011 and '13 and '15.

CHAPTER 18

SURF CAREERS

Surfing is addictive. It is also fun and amazingly rewarding, so it is only natural that many people seek to make surfing a central part of their lives. This may be as the focus of their time away from work, or an integral part of their working lives. After all, why not work in a field that you love? Modern surfing has evolved into a multi-billion pound industry, with brands, media, makers and surf schools all catering to an ever-increasing number of surfers. It is estimated there are more than 20 million surfers worldwide and more than 600,000 in the UK.

There are a number of areas within the surf industry where any number of existing skill sets are required – from designers to accountants to marketing managers. There are also a number of very specific fields where new skills are required. These can be acquired through on the job training or via courses or training programmes.

Surfing Qualifications

There is a misconception that any surfer who can rip can find a niche within the surf industry that will allow them to get the maximum amount of water time for the minimum input of work. Unfortunately those days – if they ever existed – are gone for good. Anyone seeking to work in surfing, at whatever level, requires a particular skill set, whether these are from the classroom or

A surf science degree course will teach you about the physical and geographical influences on surfing. (Photo: Sarah Bunt)

are a particular set of life skills. A strong work ethic is, needless to say, important, too. It is not by chance that of two surfers of identical talent one may have a raft of sponsors or a highly sought after job with a brand, while the other has neither.

There are now a range of surf specific qualifications on offer – from short courses for instructors in surf schools, through to three-year degrees.

The University of Plymouth began running a Surf Science and Technology degree in 1999 and now also runs a foundation level course. The course consists of a number of modules designed to give students a rounded education in all aspects of surfing, the

environment and the applicable business skills. Modules include the culture of surf, surf media and events, surf practice and production methods. Students will learn about physical and geographical influences, scientific techniques, personal and employability skills as well as social and psychology perspectives. Ecology and management of the coastal environment, scientific aspects of health, fitness and nutrition in sports are also part of the course along with aspects of business relevant to the surf industry.

Graduates have gone on to start their own surf-related companies, run marketing departments for surf brands, set up marketing and PR companies and

Another day at the office for a surf coach. (Photo: Kate Czuczman)

you an elevated profile in the surf media and images in magazines that will attract potential backers. However, that is only a small part of the job description.

Modern pros need to be media savvy, open and accessible to the press. In an age of live updates, social media and digital magazines, a sponsored rider needs to work closely with the media outlets, as well as generating his or her own content to push out to followers.

Sponsorship will come in a package with many aspects. It is rare for a surfer to be presented with a cash sum and left to his or her own devices.

There is an element of salary for living expenses and part of the package will be free product – clothing, etc. This is great for the surfer but he or she then becomes an ambassador for the brand and must be seen in the brand's clothes wherever they go. There will be a travel allowance to help attend and compete in events. There will also be a requirement to work with the brand in areas away from the sea, including product photoshoots or to attend brand

become freelance writers and photographers.

For those keen for a hands on, in the water vocation, the national governing bodies such as Surfing GB offer coaching badges for those keen to become an accredited surf coach. The recognized qualification for surf coaching in the UK is the ISA/SGB Surf Coach Level 1 award, which allows you to seek employment at hundreds of surf schools in Britain and in countries all over the world. The SGB course covers all aspects of surf education including safety, coaching techniques and group management. Successful trainees can go on to work as professional coaches, introducing beginners to the sport and helping improvers enjoy wave riding or take their surfing to the next level.

Competitive Professional Surfer

The one profession that many aspire to is that of a sponsored surfer. However,

there are a few 'qualifications needed before you begin to pull down serious money from sponsors willing to support your surfing lifestyle of travel and adventure. Firstly, you need to be able to surf to an excellent standard, with the potential of winning events. This will give

Xcel sponsored rider and free surfer Noa Deane gets paid to travel the world surfing perfect waves. (Photo: Andrew Shield/XCEL)

Pro surfer Albee Layer showing off his sponsors' logos on his board. These companies support his surfing career. (Photo: Xcel)

Free Surfer/Surf Adventurer

A surfer paid not to compete but to travel the world and score amazing waves. What's not to love? However, it's not that simple. If you're not visible at contests flying the flag for your sponsors, then why are they bankrolling you? The answer is that free surfers and surf adventurers still need to maintain a high profile in the media through films, magazine shoots, updates from trips, social media, etc.

On top of this they still need to fulfil the same criteria as a competition surfer, including product shoots and attending brand events.

Surf Media

What if you can't make it on the tour and miss out on the National Championships or just aren't a great surfer? There are still many options open that allow you to travel the world, visit some of the best waves and be involved with surf culture. Working in the surf media means writing about surfers and surfing, or documenting the surfing world through films or images.

Being a surf photographer seems like a dream job. You will tour the world with the best surfers, shoot amazing waves in stunning tropical locations and live life on the open road. This is true for many of the top lensmen and women, however as with most jobs there is more to being a surf snapper than meets the eye. Equipment is expensive, there is a lot of gear required and it is heavy to carry around. Also, there is a lot of competition so you really need to hone your photographic skills before taking the plunge. Plus, the financial rewards are hard earned. Magazines and online

promotional events or meet and greets. There may also be magazine shoots, filming trips and other projects. This can all add up to a pretty busy schedule for someone trying to crack the WSL qualifying tour.

outlets do pay, but they want the very best and unless you can score a job as a staff photographer, the freelance world can be unpredictable.

There's also the fine art of water photography. This is a real craft. Swimming out into some of the heaviest line-ups, floating inches from the impact zone, hanging in the face of a wave to catch a surfer in the optimum position takes strength, skill and the ability to read a breaking wave. Too close and you'll be either pitched over the falls or you'll be wearing a set on your head, too far away and the surfer won't be framed correctly in the curl of the wave.

However, with a good eye and practice the opportunities are there for a committed photographer. It pays to build relationships with surfers, brands and publications, then put in the practice. Of course, this means missing out on many great surf sessions – another drawback.

Many of the advantages and disadvantages faced by photographers are the same as those faced by the surf filmmaker/cameraperson – the cost of equipment, the long hours, time on the beach watching amazing surf followed by long evenings editing. However, the experiences on offer help balance this out: the travel, the chance to meet amazing people and the opportunity to be involved in producing exciting projects.

Many of the UK's top filmmakers have

The surf photographer's aim: getting his or her shot on the cover of a surf mag. (Photo: Orca)

started by producing short films on inexpensive equipment. There are many platforms for up and coming filmmakers including the London Surf/Film Festival's Shorties competition. The vision and originality of short films screened through this event have helped many filmmakers take the step up to full-time work in this field.

Surf Writer

The increase in digital platforms has provided many more opportunities for the surf creative to showcase his or her work. Online magazine sites are hungry for content or features and offer the opportunity to reach a global audience. The drawback is that there are relatively few that offer remuneration for content. For those trying to make a living in the surf media this narrows down the potential outlets.

With pressure on tradition, media such as monthly high volume magazines sold through high street outlets, there has been a shift with a number of high circulation print media going out of business while a small coterie of high quality, high price publications have sprung up in their place. Titles such as White Horses, Paper Sea Quarterly and Monster Children are less dependent on advertising due to a higher cover price and small loyal readership. They also strive for a more independent editorial line and are a good outlet for quality content for creatives.

Surf Brands

There are many opportunities to work within the surf industry, both on the sales side as well as the business and marketing side. In order to be successful it is

A good surf photographer gets really close to the action. (Photo: Ocean and Earth)

important to have the relevant skills set – after all this is primarily a business. Posts within a surf brand are always highly sought after. A good knowledge of surfing and the industry is also helpful. The wave riding world is a big family and having good social skills is a definite plus.

A highly organized person who is driven by results could consider working for a surf brand as a sales representative or agent. Larger brands will usually employ a rep who they will expect to travel around a defined area and/or work from a designated showroom. They will be expected to hit a sales target and also ensure the product is being showcased at its best in the selected stockists.

Smaller brands will use a freelance agent to sell their product; this way they only have to pay the agent a percentage of sales made and it also gives the agent the freedom to work with a portfolio of brands rather than just one.

Marketing and PR is a very broad area and can involve anything from working with budgets to planning an advertising campaign, to organising events, finding surfers to sponsor and looking after a brand's social media with an overall goal of trying to increase its presence. The job can be perceived as being great fun but also involves a lot of hard work and long hours.

Other jobs within a surf brand could be working as a designer. This includes getting involved in the creation of a particular product or the design of the marketing material to help convey the product through advertising campaigns. As with any business there are all the other important members of the team such as accountants, personal assistants, warehouse staff and delivery drivers. All are integral to the running of a successful surf company.

Surfboard Manufacturing

In the UK a good number of surfboards still come out of small factories, which employ skilled people to work on the different aspects of surfboard construction. Shaping a surfboard is considered an art and requires a number of years of shaping experience to master. Sanding, glassing and finishing are more straightforward but still require a great deal of skill and an eye for detail.

A surfboard factory will sometimes employ a young keen surfer to help sweep the floor and fix dings on damaged surfboards brought in by customers. This is a great way to learn how a surfboard is made, but be warned that surfboard factories are not the nicest of environments and a lot of unpleasant chemicals are involved in the production process.

Lifeguard

As regular water users, surfers are a natural choice for lifeguarding positions as they often possess an acute knowledge of the sea and its potential dangers. This, coupled with good all

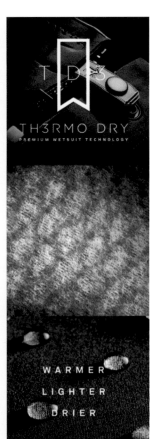
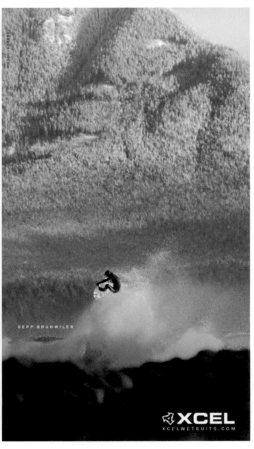

Designing for a surf brand can mean putting together adverts for magazines. (Photo: Xcel)

Surfboard shaper Ben Skinner enjoys some time out of the factory. (Photo: Sarah Bunt)

A lifeguard getting some water time while on patrol. (Photo: Sarah Bunt)

Lifeguard flags on the beach. (Photo: Sarah Bunt)

round fitness, makes them an invaluable resource for the RNLI. In the UK the lifeguarding season generally runs from May to September with the occasional week/weekend at certain beaches outside this. It is a job that holds a great deal of responsibility and requires a wide range of skills and knowledge from lifesaving to casualty care, as well as an ability to communicate well with the public.

A lifeguard needs to be incredibly fit and will be tested on his or her fitness levels throughout the lifeguarding season.

CHAPTER 19

SURF CULTURE

Modern surfing has deep roots and abundant culture that has blossomed around the fact that wave riding is a rich and diverse act. One of the central tenets has been that it is a lifestyle, not a sport. Surfing has its own history, fashion and language, all woven around the many facets of the wave riding realm. There are those who dip in and out of surfing, as one would dip in and out of golf or tennis, but for most people surfing becomes a central aspect in their lives, no matter how many times they actually manage to get in the sea. Once the bug bites, you'll always be a surfer.

Fashion

One of the earliest fashion identifiers was the Hawaiian shirt, bright and short sleeved and adorned with tropical designs including flowers, birds and palm trees. The original Hawaiian or Aloha designs were made during the 1920s for young Hawaiians in search of a leisure shirt. They were commissioned from Chinese tailors, who used spare Japanese kimono fabric, cut in a Filipino style – worn loose and designed not to be tucked in. By the 1930s Aloha shirts were produced using fabric printed with Hawaiian designs.

The surf style of clothing dates back to the earliest days of modern surfing when pioneers including Tom Blake and Duke Kahanamoku helped define the surfing aesthetic for generations to come. The blend of khaki slacks, canvas shoes and loose fit shirts set a style that is still relevant today. These early beach boys would hang at the beach in Honolulu and dress in a way that reflected their lifestyle. Baggy shorts were cheap to buy, easy to change out of and quick drying – a style of dress that continued with the North Shore pioneers of the 1950s.

When wave riding really took hold on the mainland it was primarily a counterculture and was embraced by the fringe elements of the burgeoning youth culture. They rejected the conformist nature of 1950s American consumerism and turned their backs on the rat race in favour of a 'hedonistic' lifestyle. The aim was to surf as much as possible and this meant existing on as little money as possible. The functionality of many aspects of early surf fashion reflected this: plain tees, casual chinos or jeans, and sometimes no shoes. The Aloha shirt was adopted by surfers, many of whom brought them back from trips to the islands of Hawaii.

Surfers always struggled to find swim shorts that would stay on during a wipe out and that would be durable and long lasting. In Hawaii small customized runs of surf shorts called 'drowners' were produced by tailor shops such as Minori Nii around surf spots including Makaha. Drowners became a badge of honour for California surfers, proof they'd visited the hallowed breaks of Hawaii. Legend has it that in the late 1950s up and coming California surfer Corky Carroll mentioned the lack of suitable shorts to Nancy and Walter Katin, manufacturers of canvas boat covers. They set about making Carroll a pair of custom canvas boardshorts. They were such a success that other surfers followed Corky to the Katin shop and soon everyone wanted Katin boardies. Katin became the first true surf brand, selling through the shop and then though surf shops that were springing up to feed the demand from the booming scene.

The late 1950s saw a huge surge in car sales, with Detroit marketing the latest Cadillacs, Fords and Lincolns as the lifestyle accessory, complete with yearly upgrades to keep consumers coming back year after year. Surfers, however, drove pre-war vehicles that they bought cheap from scrapyards and resurrected into surfwagons. These personalized and customized cars were an integral part of the burgeoning hot rod scene. Cars were bought cheap and these fixer-uppers were used until they broke, then taken back to the scrapyard where another candidate would be brought back to life. Surfers favoured the mechanical simplicity of cars such as the Model T and Model A Fords or the space of Woody estates – perfect for carrying surfboards and sleeping in when driving up the coast on surf trips to places including the Hollister Ranch.

Through the 1960s surf boom the

demand for boards and clothing tailored to the market exploded and a number of brands were born to satisfy this need. Hang Ten was founded in California in 1960, followed hot on its heels by Birdwell, both manufacturing boardshorts for surfers. In Australia the same process was occurring and several names that would go on to dominate global sales were soon founded. Quiksilver and Rip Curl (1969) were both founded in the small town of Torquay in Victoria. Soon surf shops were bristling with names such as Hot Tuna (1969), Ocean Pacific (1972), Billabong (1973) and many more.

In the late 1960s the influence of the Californian counterculture dovetailed with surf culture, bringing the music and fashion of the times together. Hair got longer and there was commorality in the philosophy of the rejection of mainstream society. Many surfers dropped out but this was no aimless rejection of the nine-to-five; many went in search of the perfect wave, travelling the world and pioneering some regions that westerners had yet to visit.

As the laid back 1970s merged into the frenetic 1980s the culture changed. Surfing was big business, the beaches and line-ups were bustling, and brands were multinational businesses expanding into

Surf style. (Photo: Captain Fin)

A vintage surf-inspired T-shirt. (Photo: Captain Fin)

The essentials for any aspiring surf hipster. (Photo: Captain Fin)

new markets across the globe. Europe had caught the surfing bug big time, South America followed. Neon dominated the surf look with wetsuits, boardshorts and T-shirts all glowing luminous orange, green and yellow. Brands including Hot Tuna, Gotcha, Mambo and OP blazed a bright trail with vests and baggy 'Hammer pants' in dazzling patterns, while Oakley Frogskins and Blades were the sunglasses to be seen in. Professional surfing was booming and Tom Carroll signed the sport's first million dollar contract with clothing giant Quiksilver.

During the 1990s surfing style was heavily influenced by the gravitational pull of boardsports siblings that evolved from wave riding, such as skateboarding and snowboarding. The grunge influenced look of baggy carpenter jeans/combat trousers mixed with a check lumberjack shirt was endemic through the Nirvana era of the early 1990s. This was partly a result of the musical preferences of the time but partly due to the nature of snowboarding and skate fashion with their baggy, loose-fitting style.

The tight black jeans, studded belt surf punk look was spawned from the skate boom of the mid to late 1990s. Elements of this look persist today but have split into a post-punk look as well as the current 1950s-inspired hipster style.

The surfing hipster aesthetic has its roots in modern wave riding's early days, a throwback to short back and sides haircuts, chinos, deck shoes and canvas shorts – though the products and clothing of the current movement are a long way from the cheap and functional items so revered by the pioneering surfers.

Music

One of the central tenets of surfing was that, at its core, it rejected the mainstream, ploughed its own furrow and it is that what made it so attractive to other youth elements. It meant certain bands and brands would always raid the surfing aesthetic in the hope of finding an elusive kudos.

Surf music has been a distinct genre; surfers as cultural magpies always gravitated to bands they liked, but there was no distinct musical genre that they followed wholeheartedly. Bands such as the Beach Boys seemed to associate with the beach scene as a brand, without being a sound that surfers themselves followed.

Certain bands do have a link to surf culture and a following due to the fact that the band members are themselves surfers and so relate to the culture. These include Pearl Jam, Jane's Addiction, Red Hot Chili Peppers and Reef. Other surfers include Radiohead's Thom Yorke and solo artists Jack Johnson and Ben Howard.

Films

Surf Movies in the Mainstream
The mainstream has sought to tap into the cache of surfing as a happening and relevant cultural trend, basing several Hollywood films around the lifestyle. There were a rash of Beach Blanket Bingo-style movies following on the Hawaiian shirt-tails of 1950s teen flick sensation Gidget. Every few years Hollywood attempts to recreate the success and tap into the source, with varying degrees of success.

Two of the best mainstream offerings have been helmed by surfers. The documentary Bustin' Down The Door focused on the groundbreaking and infamous Free Ride season of 1976 on the North Shore and the epic changes that reverberated around the surfing world. Produced by Shaun Tomson, it featured archive footage and intimate interviews with the main players.

Big Wednesday is a fictional feature film penned by Hollywood screenwriter and director John Milius along with surfer Denny Aaberg, and follows the lives of three surfing friends; Matt Johnson, Jack Barlow and Leroy 'The Masochist' Smith. Two of the main stars, William Katt and Jan-Michael Vincent, were already surfers, while the third lead, Gary Busy, learned quickly. The film was a critical damp squib and financial flop, but has gone on to enjoy belated success, having been rediscovered by a new generation and being lauded by critics such as Mark Kermode as one of his favourite films. It is also one of surfing's most cherished cinematic endeavours, a work that captures a period of change for not only the central characters, but also reflects the shifting tides within surf culture and the wider society at a time when the impact of the Kennedy assassination, Watergate and Vietnam heralded a loss of innocence.

Some films have gravitated from cheesy and clunky attempts to tap into surfing, mellowing with time to become endearing for all their flaws. Both Point Break and North Shore fall into this category, having become many surfers most often quoted films. Point Break was directed by Oscar-winning filmmaker Kathryn Bigelow and follows the adventures of an undercover FBI Agent, Johnny Utah, as he tries to infiltrate a gang of bank robbers known as the Ex-Presidents. The film also stars Patrick Swayze as the enigmatic Bodhie and

Surf Movies for Core Surfers

True surf movies have a rich and diverse heritage, with a vast swathe of creative and imaginative offerings that seek to capture the essence of many aspects of surf culture, from adventure to travel, from big wave riding to history. Great surf filmmakers to seek out include Bruce Brown, Bud Brown, George Greenough, Alby Falzon, Jack McCoy, Taylor Steele, Andrew Kidman, Kai Neville, Cyrus Sutton, Keith or Chris Malloy.

Classics include:
The Endless Summer
Free Ride
Crystal Voyager
Innermost Limits of Pure Fun
Morning of the Earth
Five Summer Stories
The Green Iguana
Momentum
Litmus
The September Sessions
Castles in the Sky
Thicker Than Water
Stoked and Broke
Come Hell or High Water
This Time Tomorrow
North of the Sun

George Greenough's movie Crystal Voyager has inspired kneeboarders such as Richard Hewitt. (Photo: Sarah Bunt)

Gary Busy (of *Big Wednesday*) as his FBI partner, Pappas. The film went on to gross more than $80 million.

The mediocre include *Blue Crush, Soul Surfer* and *Chasing Mavericks,* while some films are just plain bad, bypassing the fond reflections and going straight into the 'best forgotten' pile, filed under *In God's Hands.*

The annual London Surf/Film Festival is a celebration of the cream of international surf culture, showcasing the very best surf films from across the globe. Accompanied by talks from some of the most exciting wave riders from across

Will Beeslaar's creative homage to classic surf movie Morning of the Earth. (Photo: Will Beeslaar)

Surfing on the big screen at the LSFF. (Photo: LSFF/Kate Czuczman)

The audience at the LSFF enjoying the on-screen fun. (Photo: LSFF/Kate Czuczman)

A selection of surf books. (Photo: Approaching Lines)

Classic Surf Reads

Bustin' Down The Door by Tim Baker
MP, The Life of Michael Peterson by Sean Doherty
In Search of Captain Zero by Alan Weisbecker
Riding The Magic Carpet by Tom Anderson
Nat's Nat and That's That by Nat Young
All For A Few Perfect Waves by David Rensin
Caught Inside by Daniel Duane
Mr Sunset by Phil Jarrett
Fearless: The Story of Lisa Andersen by Nick Carroll
The History of Surfing by Matt Warshaw
Cold Water Souls: In Search of Surfing's Cold Water Pioneers by Chris Nelson
Surfing Europe, Surfing Britain, Surfing The World by Chris Nelson and Demi Taylor

the globe, live music and a gallery show celebrating the meeting point between surf, art and movies, it is a must attend event for surfers across the British Isles.

Books

Surfers have traditionally been great orators and storytellers – the medium has been at the heart of wave riding culture for centuries. In modern surfing the art of storytelling has gravitated from the cluster of friends in the bar or the beachside lot to the printed page. Great surf writers include Tim Baker, Nick Carroll and Sean Doherty. A good surf travel guide can also lead you to the right break for the right conditions, maximizing precious water time.

Surf Magazines

These have been an integral source of information and connection for surfers for more than fifty years. They were the main way of staying up-to-date with the sports movers and shakers long before the internet started alerting us with up to the minute reports on who had won whatever contest and who had wiped out on a massive wave somewhere on the planet.

Almost every country that has a surf community now has a plethora of surfing publications to choose from, all with a slightly different style and focus.

Surfer Magazine is the bastion of surfing, founded in 1960 in Southern California it is a wave rider's Bible with a US-centric focus that boasts an estimated audience of more than 600,000 readers. It is one of the most recognized brands in action sports and becoming a *Surfer Magazine* cover star is considered one of the highest accolades for a professional surfer. The magazine also hosts the annual Surfer-poll awards, which celebrate the world's top surfers and their achievements as voted for by readers. On its website, it has a Fantasy Surfer formula popular in mainstream sports and enables surf fans to select a

'team' of surfers and then compete against their friend's teams in 'clubs'.

Another Californian magazine, *The Surfer's Journal*, is targeted towards a slightly more mature reader who is looking for a publication that they can keep and archive for future reference and enjoyment. It relies on brands to 'sponsor' the magazine rather than advertising in it and demands a higher cover price due to its premium quality.

ASL, STAB and *Tracks* are Australian publications with an irreverent slant on

UK surf magazine Carve. (Photo: Orca)

Surfgirl *magazine features female surfers from the UK and all over the world. (Photo: Orca)*

Surfers of all ages love practising tricks that they've seen photos of in their favourite mags. (Photo: Sarah Bunt)

the varying faces of surf culture. Using classic Aussie humour to navigate around the surfing arena they offer a different perspective to their American counterparts and are happy to poke fun at themselves along the way. *Foam Symmetry* focuses on Australia's alternative surf scene and features photographs and articles with surfers riding a multitude of different wave riding craft from logs to single fins and mini-simmons to alaias.

Carve Magazine has been a mainstay of British surfing since its inception in 1994. With nine issues per year its UK perspective makes it a great resource for surfers from these shores, enabling them to get a flavour of the global surf scene but through British eyes. In 2003 it launched a sister publication, *Surfgirl*, that takes a female slant on the scene, covering everything that interests and inspires female surfers.

The UK's longest standing surf publication is *Wavelength*. With more than thirty years in print, it has stood the test of time when other magazines have come and gone. In this time it has had many guises but has always remained at the forefront of British surfing.

There are several other publications available that are not pure surf mags but give a nod to surfing along with travel, art and other interests that inspire their readers to create and explore. These include Australian magazines *White Horses* and *Paper Sea Quarterly*, and *Huck* magazine from the UK.

Online Media

Surfers spend a lot time on the internet, either shopping for an essential piece of surf kit, catching one of the pro's latest edits or checking the surf report for their local beach. Forecasting sites such as MagicSeaweed are a one-stop shop for every keen surfer. With a few clicks of the mouse, they can check the swell for this weekend's waves, see a clip of their favourite surfer pulling into a perfect barrel and purchase a set of fins just like the ones that same surfer is using.

The Inertia and Korduroy.TV are go-to sites to read interesting articles where various contributors share their surf-related knowledge and opinions. These sites are great platforms for aspiring writers and creators to get their work and musings out to an audience of information-hungry surf fans.

CHAPTER 20

ALTERNATIVE WAVECRAFT

There are many forms of wave riding that fall under the surfing umbrella, and today surfers embrace a wide spectrum of craft, depending on conditions. Pioneering surfer Phil Edwards said 'the best surfer out there is the one having the most fun' – and having a range of wave riding vehicles in a quiver ensures you'll be having the most fun on any given day.

Bodysurfing/ Handplanes

Bodysurfing is probably the most ancient form of wave riding. It is certainly the most basic, yet most revered of all the surfing disciplines. Bodysurfing requires skill and technique, and an understanding of waves and the ocean. Most bodysurfers simply require a pair of swim fins to catch and ride waves. As a wave approaches and begins to pitch, a body surfer paddles into the wave using the propulsion of the swim fins by kicking their legs. Some may also use a single or double arm paddle too. Once the wave begins to pitch, the body surfer is propelled forward by the wave and can trim across the face, hanging in the steepest part of the curl, their body acting as a flexible 'surfboard' with the trailing fin acting as a rail.

With a little practice a bodysurfer can get into the hollowest part of the wave, getting barrelled on some of the smallest

Handplaning is surfing in its purest form. (Photo: Sarah Bunt)

Bodysurfing kit. (Photo: Approaching Lines)

days as well as some of the biggest.

Many bodysurfers also use a handplane – a small wooden surfboard-shaped plane with a neoprene and Velcro strap to prevent it from being lost. The plane works like a surfboard in that it provides lift and acts as a planning surface, allowing the bodysurfer to push

down on to the plane and decrease the drag of the body in the wave face. It also aids trim in the face and turning.

Bodysurfing is a great skill to master and helps all-round water knowledge. It has always been popular with the legendary Hawaiian lifeguards such as Mark Cunningham as well as renowned

No board, no worries – a bodysurfer perfectly in tune with the wave. (Photo: Sarah Bunt)

trim waves of all sizes in all kinds of conditions. A bellyboard can transform a small onshore day when a surfboard may prove to be frustrating.

There is an annual World Bellyboard Championship held each autumn in Cornwall, offering all comers the chance to compete for the crown of world champion. There are several modern Bellyboard brands including Original Surfboard Company and Traditional Surfing.

Paipo

The paipo is a traditional Hawaiian wave riding craft, short in length and ridden prone. Recently the paipo has been rediscovered and reinterpreted by a raft

watermen such as Mike Stewart. It is also great when travelling without a surfboard as if there are waves, it is always possible to get in and catch a few.

Bellyboard

This is a form of wave riding that dates back to the early twentieth century and was popular at UK coastal resorts. A bellyboard is made from plywood with a rounded front that has rocker – or lift – in the nose. Holidaymakers would stand in waist deep water and push off into the whitewater and ride the waves prone to the beach.

Modern bellyboarders have taken these humble craft out into the line-up and with the use of fins can catch and

Surf photographer Mat Arney with his paipo. (Photo: Approaching Lines)

Bellyboarding attracts waveriders of all ages. (Photo: Sarah Bunt)

Competitors at the National Trust World Bellyboarding Championships running in for their heat. (Photo: Sarah Bunt)

of makers across the globe. There is a new generation riding everything from traditional koa paipos to carbon fibre, asymmetric paipo spoons. These types of boards are ridden prone with fins and are becoming increasingly popular. There are a number of makers handcrafting wooden paipos, including Paipo Glide and SAW Boards.

Alaia

The traditional Hawaiian alaia is a thin wooden board between 7 and 12ft in length with a flat rocker and sharp rails. It is relatively narrow and finless, making it difficult to master but great fun to ride. Its low volume makes catching waves much harder than with a foam shortboard. The modern use of the alaia was pioneered by surfboard shaper Tom Wegener, who produces a number of designs based on the traditional wooden form using light and strong paulownia wood.

The principles of the alaia are also being translated into new designs in soft foam plus polyurethane foam and fibreglass, offering a more accessible form of fins-free wave riding. These designs include the Albacore and the Seaglass Tuna. They catch waves like a conventional surfboard but lack fins, allowing the board to be rotated through 360 degrees while maintaining a forward motion across the face of the wave.

The modern form of fins-free surfing was pioneered by surf maverick and former professional Derek Hynd. He coined the phrase 'Far Field Free Friction' for this style of wave riding. Hynd has a variety of foam boards in his quiver, experimenting with both asymmetric designs and channel bottoms.

Surfmat

The surfmat is a design dating back to the Second World War – an inflatable ribbed mat used to ride waves. Early designs were rigid and heavy, but surfing pioneers such as George Greenough customized their mats by peeling the canvas from the bottom to reveal the more pliable thin rubber skin (these mats were affectionately known as peelers). Those peelers would eventually pick up leaks, leading to an interesting discovery: mats work best when they are made from pliable fabrics and run at low inflation. While the rest of the prone world was pushing the boundaries on foam, a small band of mat builders were exploring the possibilities of inflation or, more accurately, deflation and pliability.

One of the most significant breakthroughs came when Oregon's Dale Solomonson began using high grade, lightweight, weldable nylon. At this point the direction and definition of the surfmat was changed forever. Dale, Paul Gross and George worked closely together, quickly blowing their way through hundreds of yards of fabric perfecting the modern mat. Dale went on to create custom surfmats under the Neumatic label and Paul launched Fourth Gear Flyer. Their ongoing hard work saw a core group of mat riders take their art on to a completely new

Custom built G-Mat surfmats. (Photo: Approaching Lines)

level, finding previously unexplored levels of speed and performance.

Today, surfmats might have a low profile but the truth is they definitely are out there, and the crew that ride them have a refreshingly simple attitude – you could say their egos are like their mats, under-inflated.

Bodyboard

Taking inspiration from the traditional forms of wave riding, the bodyboard was first manufactured in 1971 by Tom Morey, who was trying to create a foam surfboard with a slick bottom. When his original prototype was snapped in half by a breaking wave, Morey was determined to make something rideable from a remaining piece of foam. He sliced it in half with a knife and the bodyboard was born.

Designed to be surfed while wearing swim fins, the construction today still consists of a foam deck and plastic bottom encasing a foam core, all bonded together using a hot air lamination technique. The correct amount of flex that a bodyboard has is crucial to it maintaining speed. The curve of the board can vary from one model to another depending on whether the rider prefers to ride lying down (prone) or with the fin on their front foot flat on their board and the fin on their back foot trailing in the water (dropknee).

The sport's most successful competitor is Hawaiian Mike Stewart; with nine world titles he is considered the father of modern bodyboarding. Brazilian Stephanie Petterson was the first female world champion, winning the event at Pipeline in Hawaii in 1990.

Bodyboarder Marcus Read showing his skills. (Photo: Sarah Bunt)

Stand Up Paddleboard

Although the concept of standing up on a board and using a paddle to propel yourself forward has been around for centuries, the modern form of SUP'ng is actually the most recent addition to the wave riding community. However, judging by its high uptake rate it is destined to stick around, especially as it offers an alternative option when the waves are small.

The majority of SUPs are constructed of glass-reinforced plastic, are around 9ft in length and the paddles are of carbon construction. However, there are many variations depending on personal preference and the conditions that the SUPs are used in. Inflatable boards are a popular option due to the ease with

Stand up paddleboarding is growing rapidly in popularity. (Photo: Sarah Bunt)

ALTERNATIVE WAVECRAFT

Jimbo Bennett dropping into a wave on his finless Albacore. (Photo: Approaching Lines/Mat Arney)

which they can be transported around. The current stand up world champion is Kai Lenny. Hailing from the island of Maui, Lenny took up stand up paddleboarding at the age of 7 after learning to surf at age 4 and windsurf at 6. As with many professional SUP-ers he is a skilled waterman who competes in a variety of different surfing disciplines.

Surfmat riders heading into the water at the Slyder Cup. (Photo: Approaching Lines/Mat Arney)

CHAPTER 21

SURF CLUBS

Surf clubs are important community hubs that allow local water users to make use of their beachside facilities and take part in various inter-club events. These member only organisations can either take the form of the original Surf Life Saving Clubs with a focus on beach safety or Boardriders clubs that are more surfing-specific. Some clubs will cater for both. Joining a surf club will require paying a membership fee but this will allow you to use the facilities, which could include hot showers – a real treat after a cold winter surf.

History and Function

Surf Life Saving Clubs came into existence in the early 1900s in Sydney, Australia, as residents in the eastern suburbs of the city felt there was a need to educate people in lifesaving techniques after it was noted that a number of people were getting into difficulty while bathing off the beaches close by.

In 1907 the Surf Bathing Association of New South Wales was founded and this became the governing body to which the then increasing number of clubs popping up in the state could affiliate. This later became Surf Life Saving Australia (SLSA), which is now responsible for providing the national lifeguard service, educating the wider community about beach safety and researching possible new safety initiatives. The SLSA also organizes the national Surf Life Saving championships where club members can showcase their lifesaving skills through different disciplines including ocean swimming, paddle boarding and surf ski paddling.

Today there are more than 300 surf lifesaving clubs in Australia and, as well as running lifesaving courses for all ages, many have diversified into becoming venues for weddings and various community-based functions.

Almost all Australia's most popular surfing beaches have their own Boardriders' clubs that aim to help aspiring young surfers on their journey to hopefully joining the professional ranks by giving them the necessary training and support. Boardriders' clubs will compete to become the national champions and will submit teams into the state qualifiers, with the top twenty teams going on to compete in the national finals. These regularly draw in the big names from the WCT, including the likes of Tyler Wright (Culburra Beach Boardriders Club) and Joel Parkinson (Snapper Rocks Surfriders Club), who have both competed in the event in the past.

Sea swimming is integral to being a surf club member. (Photo: Sarah Bunt)

Surf Clubs in the UK

In the UK, Surf Life Saving and Boardriders' clubs are lower key affairs. Of the forty-plus surf clubs in the UK, one of the longest surviving is Portreath Surf Lifesaving Club. Set up in 1958, again as the result of a number of people getting into difficulty while bathing there, it is one of the country's most successful, with a strong membership and back catalogue of competitive success. It is affiliated, along with the other UK's surf clubs, to Surf Life Saving GB, which mirrors the work of its Australian equivalent.

There are a number of Boardriders' clubs across the UK. Some follow the Australian structure and are based at a specific beach while others such as British Bodyboard Club and The British

Many of the UK's lifeguards learn their skills at their local surf club. (Photo: Sarah Bunt)

Paddleboarding is one of the disciplines that is taught at surf clubs. (Photo: Sarah Bunt)

Longboard Union have members that are unified by the type of craft that they ride rather than the beach where they surf. Some, such as Bristol Surf Club were started to help surfers based in the city get together to share the costs of travelling to the beach.

The British Interclub Championships, held at different locations each year are an opportunity for Boardriders clubs from around the UK to compete against each other by submitting teams consisting of male, female and junior surfers.

FURTHER INFORMATION

Competitions and governing bodies

BLU Longboard Tour –
www.british-longboard-union.co.uk

English Surfing Federation –
www.englishsurfing.co.uk

European Championships –
www.eurosurfing.org

Girls Ten Board Challenge –
www.facebook.com/tenboardchallenge

ISA World Surfing Games –
www.isasurf.org

Scottish Surfing Federation –
www.thessf.com

The Slyder Cup –
www.approachinglines.com

Swellboard Shootout –
www.stivessurfschool.co.uk/swellboard -shootout-2014

UK Professional Surf Tour –
www.ukprosurf.com

Welsh Surfing Federation –
www.welshsurfingfederation.org.uk

World Surf League –
www.worldsurfleague.com

Environment and campaign groups

Marine Conservation Society –
www.mcsuk.org.

Surfers Against Sewage –
www.sas.org.uk

Surfrider Foundation –
www.surfrider-europe.org

2 Minute Beach Clean –
www.beachclean.net

Fitness and exercise

Helen Clare yoga classes and retreats –
www.helenclareyoga.com

SwimLab –
www.swimlab.org.uk

INDEX

OTHER SPORTS GUIDES FROM CROWOOD

978 1 84797 959 9

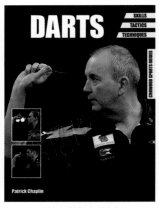

978 1 78500 005 8

978 1 84797 531 7

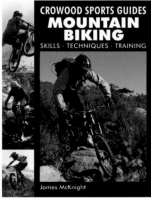

978 1 84797 419 8

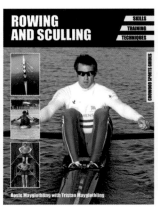

978 1 84797 746 5

978 1 84797 520 1

978 1 84797 256 9

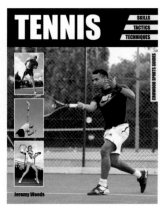

978 1 84797 748 9

978 1 84797 170 8